PHOTO: KARSH

Front cover: Nancy Barrow played the title role in the 1935 production of Maxwell Anderson's *Elizabeth the Queen*, directed by Dorothy White.

Back cover: The great fire of July 1, 1970 destroyed the building but not the spirit of Ottawa Little Theatre.

Author photo: J.M. Carisse

Overleaf: Charles McConkey in the 1934 production of *Tobias and the Angel* by James Bridie, directed by Rupert Harvey.

Staging a Legend

A History of Ottawa Little Theatre

by

Iris Winston

Published by Creative Bound Inc.
151 Tansley Drive
P.O. Box 424
Carp, Ontario K0A 1L0
(613) 831-3641

ISBN 0-921165-49-8
Printed and bound in Canada

Book design by Wendelina O'Keefe

Canadian Cataloguing in Publication Data

Winston, Iris
Staging a legend : a history of Ottawa Little Theatre

Includes bibliographical references.
ISBN 0-921165-49-8

1. Ottawa Little Theatre—History. I. Title.

PN3169.C32O88 1997 792'.0222'0971384 C97-900631-7

For Sybil

The history of the Theatre is bound up with the history of Ottawa, because it is the people of Ottawa who have supported it so loyally over the years and have enabled it to carry on.

Dorothy White

It is really a club which anyone who is interested can join and provides an outlet for all those whose hobby is the theatre.

Elizabeth Cruikshank

Acknowledgements

My sincere thanks to the many people who have generously given of their time to share their memories and so trustingly lent me treasured photographs, programs and other momentoes:

Bert Adkins, Audrey Ashley, Janet Banigan, Valentine Barrow, Kenneth Binks, Jim Bishop, Val Bogan, Beatrice Brace, Marian Bray, Kevin and Elizabeth Conlon, Douglas and Sybil Cooke, Florence Fancott, Pamela Fish, Leonie Gardner, Charles Haines, Yousuf Karsh, Miriam Lewis, Bill Luxton, Barbara Meiklejohn, Lorraine St. Laurent, Phyllis Ullrich, Tsin Van, Michael Vuckovic, Dick and Wallis White.

Special thanks to my favourite reference librarian, Joni Waiser, and also to Elizabeth Holden, Tom Pidgeon and the staff of Ottawa Little Theatre for all their help.

RIDEAU HALL
OTTAWA

THE GOVERNOR GENERAL
LE GOUVERNEUR GÉNÉRAL

Theatre companies, small and large, play a vital role in the cultural life of communities. The Ottawa Little Theatre is an important part of that tradition. It has been on the leading edge of theatre in Canada for most of this century – the first community theatre, the first home of the Dominion Drama Festival, and the host of a national playwriting competition for Canadians. Over the years, the Ottawa Little Theatre has helped to promote aspiring Canadian writers and actors, and has taught thousands of people to love plays, from farces to dramas.

In some ways, the history of the Ottawa Little Theatre mirrors that of the Ottawa region and the entire country. The Ottawa Little Theatre struggled to come into its own in the early part of this century, just as Canada was developing into an independent nation. Its membership was inevitably affected by war and economic depression. Over the years, as Canada prospered, the Ottawa Little Theatre has also flourished on the Ottawa arts scene.

From the time Lord Bessborough designed sets for it in the 1930s, the Ottawa Little Theatre has had a close relationship with the Governor General, and I am pleased to be part of this tradition. I am sure that everyone who has been associated with the theatre will enjoy and treasure this book.

Roméo LeBlanc

Roméo LeBlanc

August 1997

Staging a Legend

A History of Ottawa Little Theatre

Contents

Introduction

I first heard a passing reference to Ottawa Little Theatre in 1965. A television announcer happened to mention that it was the first home of the Dominion Drama Festival as part of his introduction to the broadcast of that year's festival. The program caught my interest. I was a new Canadian, in my first year of teaching high school in a small community on the south shore of Nova Scotia, anxious to learn more about Canada. As a long-time theatre enthusiast, I was even more interested in learning about theatre in Canada.

From an early age, I had haunted the cheap seats of my local theatre in southwest London. Most Saturday afternoons, I invested around fifty cents (half my weekly allowance) on a seat in the second balcony of the Streatham Hill Theatre to see previews of shows destined for London's West End. Later, there were trips to the West End theatres themselves. In between, I was involved in school productions and the local amateur dramatic society. Theatre in general, community theatre in particular, were part of the fabric of my formative years.

So it was that in 1965, that casual mention of Ottawa Little Theatre caught my attention. The next year, I moved to Calgary, several thousand kilometres away. Once more, I heard about Ottawa Little Theatre. This time, it was a note in a newspaper column, soliciting submissions for the theatre's one-act playwriting competition. An amateur theatre group sponsoring a playwriting competition? It was becoming clear that Ottawa Little Theatre was no ordinary community theatre.

Some twenty years later, I was living in Saskatoon and had just been made Communications Director of Persephone Theatre. The artistic director, Tibor Feheregyhazi, was justifiably proud of the attractive facility on the city's west side. When I complimented him on the building, he explained that it was modelled on his *alma mater*, Ottawa Little Theatre. There was Ottawa Little Theatre again, in yet another part of the country.

Tibor, a professional actor in his native Hungary, joined Ottawa Little Theatre in 1956, a refugee to Canada following the revolution there. He began rebuilding his life in Ottawa, sweeping hospital floors by day and walking the boards of the theatre at night. And he took the image of Ottawa Little Theatre's "new" building—the theatre that rose from the ashes of the old building destroyed by fire in 1970—with him when he eventually moved west to head professional theatres, first in Thunder Bay and later in Saskatoon.

When I finally saw my first play at Ottawa Little Theatre in 1989, the building felt familiar. I even spotted Tibor's photograph among the hundreds of images of actors, directors and designers that grace the foyer. I knew already that Ottawa Little Theatre was a special place that had had an extraordinary influence on the dramatic life of the country, far beyond the geographic boundaries of Ottawa. I was to find out how many professional actors had begun their careers here, how the theatre had grown with the city and just what an important part of Ottawa's cultural life it had been since 1913.

There's a story to tell about Ottawa Little Theatre. I am pleased to have the chance to tell it.

CHAPTER 1

The Beginnings

...nature's handmaid art
Makes mighty things from small beginnings grow.
John Dryden in *Annus Mirabilis*

Perhaps the catalyst for Ottawa Little Theatre's small beginning was one aspiring actor's dream of playing Lady Macbeth. Perhaps it was a more scholarly wish to analyse plays or to create "audiences who were educated in their appreciation and discrimination regarding dramatic productions."[1] Reasons may have varied, but the seed of Canada's oldest community theatre group was planted when the University Women's Club[2] invited "Milton Rosmer (of Miss Horniman's company of Manchester Players) to address an open meeting in the Normal School."[3] On May 9, 1913, "a number of men and women of the Capital gathered to discuss the formation of a Drama League."[4] This group, originally called the Society for the Study and Production of Dramatic Art, was to become the first Canadian branch of the Drama League of America.[5] It grew very quickly, boasting some two hundred members by the end of its first year.

The birth of the Drama League of America's newest branch was even noted in the British press. British journalist Edward Spence commented in the August 2,

---

1. "Ottawa Drama League—Early History" by E. Arma Smillie, M.A. in *Canadian Bookman*, Vol. 5, 1923, p. 151. Ms. Smillie was a member of the committee of the University Women's Club, instrumental in founding the League in 1913.
2. The University Women's Club was a group of women with degrees from various universities. It was not associated with a single university.
3. "Ottawa Drama League—Early History," *op. cit.*, p. 151.
4. *Ottawa Journal*, January 5, 1928, p. 11, from a story on the opening of the theatre building.
5. "The Ottawa Little Theatre—Past and Present" by Alison Taylor Hardy in *The Curtain Call*, January 1941, Vol. 12, No. 4, p. 3. *The Curtain Call* was the official publication of the Dominion Drama Festival.

1913 issue of the *Westminster Gazette*: "I hear that a branch has just been born in Ottawa. I noticed with interest that not only was the League founded by women, but a large number of its officials belong to that sex. American women are supposed to be prudish and it might be feared that under the circumstances and the working of the League, though it would operate against the simply erotic forms of entertainment, [it] would also follow the lines of our [British] censorship and exhibit an extravagant terror of indelicacy in the treatment of serious subjects."[6]

Not so, says Arma Smillie, a member of the drama group's founding committee:

> *From the beginning, the aims of the league were to insure a good attendance at the deserving plays which were bulletined from the American headquarters a few weeks in advance of their production....Unworthy plays were not condemned by bulletins, but ignored....At first [the Ottawa Drama League] was a branch of the Drama League of America, which was most helpful in its assistance...later, when the war made the aims of the two somewhat divergent, it became an independent society, purely Canadian. It [was] now affiliated with the British Drama League, and in friendly alliance with the American.*
>
> *The Dramatic Committee directed the performance of plays....Well-known actors were entertained or lectured to us, and teas and addresses were both well-attended, the outstanding one being that by F.R. Benson and Archibald Flower, of the Stratford-on-Avon Theatre.*[7]

"The first president was Mr. Sykes (W. J. Sykes, head of the Carnegie Library) and the first vice-president was Miss Ada Baker from the University Women's Club. Mrs. Madge Macbeth was the second president. She had acted professionally in the United States, had seen the beginning of the Little Theatre Movement there, and believed Ottawa could successfully operate a Little Theatre. She threw the enthusiasm so characteristic of her into the movement here and worked very hard for it in those formative years."[8]

6. As quoted by Alison Taylor Hardy in "The Ottawa Little Theatre—Past and Present," *op.cit.*
7. "Ottawa Drama League—Early History," *op. cit.*, p. 151.
8. *Ottawa's Heritage of Theatre (1837-1955)* by Mrs. Roy McGregor Watt, Bytown Pamphet Series, No. 5, p. 11. Mrs. Watt was a staunch member of the Ottawa Drama League, who worked particularly hard to promote its One-Act Playwriting Competition. Her many years of hard work were recognized when she was awarded the Order of Canada in 1973. Two other members, Bill Adkins and Jane Murray, were also inducted into the Order of Canada in recognition of their services to theatre.

The combination of an energetic president and the group's outgrowing its book-club approach to drama soon changed its focus. The ladies and gentlemen of the League recognized that theatre is a living, breathing art form and that plays are written to be performed rather than read.

On November 15, 1913, they presented three one-act plays (by G.K. Chesterton, John Synge and Stanley Houghton) at the Russell Theatre on Queen and Elgin Streets (close to where the National Arts Centre was erected in 1969.)[9] Two years later, the expanded Ottawa Drama League had become a *bona fide* community theatre group ready to present its first play in the auditorium of the Victoria Memorial Museum (today, the Canadian Museum of Nature) on MacLeod Street. The move to the museum theatre was treated as a matter of some significance in the country's theatrical development:

> *The Canadian Government has done an extraordinary thing...it has made the most radical movement towards national art that has ever taken place in the Dominion...It has handed over, lock, stock and barrel a beautiful auditorium in the Victoria Memorial Museum to the Drama League of Ottawa for production and fostering Canadian drama.*[10]

Playwright Harley Granville-Barker—later to become adjudicator of the yet unborn Dominion Drama Festival—presided at the Ottawa Drama League's opening ceremony at the museum theatre. There, the following year, the group presented *The Suffragist* by Ottawa playwright Dr. Donald Guthrie. A Canadian play by a Canadian playwright, performed by Canadian actors, it was a landmark in the nation's theatrical growth.

The Ottawa Drama League had already made its mark as part of Canada's burgeoning little theatre movement. "While we possessed this little theatre home, we made the best possible use of it," writes Arma Smillie. "At Christmas time that year, our Junior League, trained by Mrs. Macbeth, put on *While the Chimes Rang*, on two evenings; ...In January Arnold Bennett's *Honeymoon* was given, both in our own theatre and, by special request, in the Balderson Theatre, Perth, Ontario."[11]

9. The Russell Theatre was demolished in 1937 to make way for the approach to Confederation Square. A delegation to Prime Minister William Lyon Mackenzie King had petitioned for the building and its theatre tradition to be saved. The delegation could not save the theatre, but was promised that a national theatre would be built to take its place.
10. From a report by columnist Beverly Baxter, quoted in *Ottawa's Heritage of Theatre (1837-1955), op. cit.*, p. 12, and in "The Ottawa Little Theatre—Past and Present" by Alison Taylor Brady in *The Curtain Call, op.cit.*
11. "Ottawa Drama League—Early History," *op. cit.*, p. 151.

A year later, however, the group suffered its first major setback. It lost its newly acquired home after a major fire destroyed the main Parliament building in 1916 and the House of Commons relocated in the museum while it was being rebuilt. "Our theatre was dismantled, our scenery removed, and the curtain rose on the Canadian Political Drama instead."[12]

The League's membership had also dropped after the outbreak of World War I. "We lost by enlistment several of our executive and many members," reports Arma Smillie.

> *Several of our members were in active dramatic societies behind the firing line throughout the war, and the membership dropped to forty-nine, where it remained for quite a while. The future outlook seemed very dark, and many advised us to let the league die, but the more courageous decided that we could continue to exist if we did so for unselfish purposes. Accordingly, we announced our intention to put on plays for patriotic purposes alone, and showed our willingness to assist others in this work. So we kept alive.*[13]

Over the next seven years, the group, performing at the Russell Theatre, showed that it had established strong enough roots to survive. "Relying on the restoration of our home when circumstances would permit, we carried on," says Miss Smillie. And carry on the League did, with some success. It was during this period that the junior division celebrated the Shakespearean tercentenary by presenting *Master Will of Stratford*[14] at the Russell, "to such a crowded house that the police interfered and the performance had to be repeated for those turned away."[15]

By 1923, the group, now once again with a membership of more than two hundred, was back in the museum and producing a regular season of plays, rather than mounting occasional shows. "Public opinion seemed to think we filled a long-felt want in Ottawa dramatic circles," says Miss Smillie. "Those who carried on through these trying years are now seeing their faith justified, for since the return to the 'Little Theatre' our membership has jumped to seven hundred....Now we must await the judgment of the future as to the worth...of these our ten year's *[sic]* efforts."16

12. *Ibid.*
13. *Ibid.*
14. A young Eugene Forsey, now Senator Forsey, played the lead, reports Valentine Barrow in "The Ottawa Little Theatre: A Brief History," a paper written for the University of Victoria, April 3, 1984.
15. "Ottawa Drama League—Early History," *op. cit.*
16. *Ibid.*

Miss Smillie would have been pleased as the conjunction of two events cemented the theatre group's future. The first was the flowering of community theatre across the country. The second was the installation of an Ottawa Drama League president, Dr. Duncan Campbell Scott,[17] who was determined to give the group a permanent home.

The period between the two world wars was truly the golden age of little theatre, which grew mightily as commercial theatre of the period declined with the development of radio and movies. Hundreds of community theatre groups sprang up across the country. They ranged from a few people coming together to mount one play for a single performance to a company organized to present a regular season of plays in its own theatre.

At that time, the Ottawa Drama League fell somewhere between the two. It was well enough established to present a season of plays in the same location, but it did not have a home of its own. Past experience had made it clear that a theatre group simply leasing a space was in a precarious position. Permanence could be assured only if the Ottawa Drama League had its own theatre.

The
Ottawa Drama League Incorporated
MORTGAGE BOND

$25.00 Serial A..........

No. 137

1. The OTTAWA DRAMA LEAGUE INCORPORATED for value received hereby promises to pay to the registered holder for the time being hereof or his registered legal representatives, or assigns, at the office of the Toronto General Trusts Corporation, in the City of Ottawa, on or before the third day of January, 1958, the sum of Twenty-five ($25.00) dollars of lawful money of Canada together with interest thereon at the rate of four per cent in accordance with the terms of a certain deed of trust to secure an issue of bonds of which this bond is one, the said deed being dated the twenty-fifth day of November, 1927, and registered in the Registry Office, for Registry Division, the City of Ottawa in the County of Carleton in the Province of Ontario on the 1st day of December, 1927, as No. 190433.

This Bond shall not become obligatory until certified by the Trustee under said Deed of Trust, upon the certificate endorsed hereon.

IN WITNESS WHEREOF the seal of the OTTAWA DRAMA LEAGUE INCORPORATED has been hereunder affixed under the hands of the duly authorized officers of this third day of January, 1928.

President.

Secretary.

A few years before, that might have seemed an impossible dream. But with the ever-increasing interest in community theatre across the country and the determination of Duncan Campbell Scott, League president from 1923 to 1936, vice-presidents Colonel Henry Osborne and Dorothy White, and fundraising chair Elizabeth (Mrs. Dwight P.) Cruickshank, the dream was to become reality.

17. "Whenever Duncan Campbell Scott said something you jumped," says Bert Adkins, son of Bill Adkins, long-time Ottawa Little Theatre stage manager, appointed by Dr. Scott, when the Ottawa Drama League was still performing in the museum.

The League set up its campaign headquarters in an office on Wellington Street. By 1926, leaflets calling for donations to a $60,000 building fund appeared all over the city and non-interest-bearing mortgage bonds were being sold at $25 apiece. "We wanted more than 600 people to donate so that there would be a real foundation of interest within the community," recalled Elizabeth (Betty) Cruikshank in 1969. "Many people bought three or four."[18] They also bought the "horrible little stuffed dogs"[19] that she made for sale whenever Ottawa Drama League board members spoke at fundraising meetings.

"We've had all kinds of strange homes," Colonel Osborne said at one of these meetings. "Parish halls, obscure rooms, the Museum theatre. Now we want a theatre as good as Hart House in Toronto."[20]

Two years later, the group had its wish. The Ottawa Drama League had raised enough money to buy an old church property: the Eastern Methodist Church on the corner of King Edward Avenue and Besserer Street (closed at the time of the union of the Presbyterian, Methodist and Congregational Churches in Canada in 1925). The group went on to raise the money to convert the building into a theatre and, on January 3, 1928, the auditorium was officially opened by the Governor General, Freeman Freeman-Thomas, Marquess of Willingdon. "When Lord Willingdon parted the beautiful stage curtains on that significant evening...his words expressed pride of achievement and rang with prophecy for nation-wide achievement. He said: 'It may be said that this is a small beginning, but let us always

The Eastern Methodist Church at the corner of King Edward Avenue and Besserer Street that was to become Ottawa Little Theatre.

18. From an interview with Sheila McCook, *Ottawa Citizen*, August 6, 1969.
19. *Ibid.*
20. As reported in *Love and Whisky* by Betty Lee, McClelland and Stewart Ltd., 1973, p. 79, and in Ottawa Little Theatre scrapbook.

remember that small beginnings very often produce big endings and I venture to express the confident hope that the example you are setting today will be rapidly followed and that our federal capital city may become in future years the great centre for encouragement of all the finer arts and crafts'."[21]

> *The President and Directors of*
>
> **The Ottawa Drama League**
>
> Request your Attendance on the Afternoon
>
> *of*
>
> TUESDAY, JANUARY 3rd, 1928
>
> *at* HALF-PAST FOUR O'CLOCK
>
> when His Excellency the Governor General
> will open the Little Theatre
> King Edward Avenue and Besserer Street
>
> R. S. V. P. — To the Secretary of the Drama League P.O. Box 604

The pride of both the group and the city at large was reflected in the headline of a January 3, 1928 advertising feature in the *Ottawa Journal*, which announced that "Ottawa's New Little Theatre is the Largest and Best Equipped of its Kind in Canada." It continued:

> *Distinct advances have been made in the arts of drama, music and literature in Ottawa within the past few years. This pronounced development has been widespread throughout the city, with increased attention to amateur theatricals, the concert stage, instrumental music, music in the homes, more and better books and entertainment features generally. Marked improvements in musical instruments and improved radio programs have had a share in popularizing the arts among all classes.*
>
> ***Artistic Improvement is Desired***
>
> *For many residents of the Capital, literature and music have reached a truly substantial stage, and the refining influence of artistic development is evident on all sides. The people are actually becoming earnest patrons of music and amateur drama in large numbers and of book-lovers there are legion. Knowledge of these arts is rapidly spreading, and there is a sincere desire for the enjoyment of artistic atmosphere in personal activities and social pursuits. The memory of good music, the reading of a good book and the enjoyment of a well-acted play all tend toward happy and substantial life.*

21. *Ottawa's Heritage of Theatre (1837-1955), op. cit.*, p. 13.

Advance in Amateur Presentations

One of the impressive developments in the realm of theatricals in recent years has been the "Little Theatre" movement, constituting a substantial advance in amateur dramatic art. Ottawa is now in the forefront in this trend through the establishment of a "Little Theatre" having all of the comforts and equipment of a large professional dramatic palace. This is now ready, after weeks of careful preparation, for the formal opening, Tuesday afternoon, January 3 at 4:30 o'clock, by his Excellency the Governor-General. The first presentation in the theatre will be given by the Ottawa Drama League on Wednesday evening, January 4, this being "Anthony and Anna."

Patrons of amateur drama in Ottawa will find the interior of the Little Theatre a work of art in itself. The structure has been remodelled for the purposes of dramatic offerings at a cost which is close to $75,000 and the very best thought has been put into the many new details. The playhouse is situated at the corner of King Edward Avenue and Besserer Street, with the handsome new entrance on King Edward Avenue.

Foyer is Place of Distinct Beauty

Passing through the stone doorway, one finds himself in the lobby, where the box office and other facilities are located, creating an atmosphere in keeping with the presentations that are to be enjoyed. The foyer, which is literally one of the finest in Canada, has ample dimensions, being 75 feet long and 35 feet wide. Possessing an early Venetian motif with curved stone pillars, great open fireplace and gorgeous stained glass windows, one feels an invitation to linger.

Combine Comfort and Beauty

The auditorium itself is also beautiful to behold. Overhead is the attractive, blue vaulted ceiling with handsomely carved beams, while on the floor are the 498 opera chairs, appropriately spaced for comfort and richly furnished in deep leather upholstery. Wide aisles give easy access to all parts of the house and every seat will be found acceptable in the matter of stage view and acoustics.

The large stage is framed in a wonderful proscenium arch having a polychrome decorative effect. Below it is the spacious orchestra pit with conductor's platform and all other musical essentials. The stage is 75 feet wide and 30 feet deep, ample room for all presentations. All contrivances of modern statecraft have been installed, these including an up-to-date electrical switchboard and complete equipment for all desired lighting effects. There is an extensive array of scenery, curtains, back drops and stage properties, insuring the proper settings for types of performances. Back stage are found ample dressing rooms, a green room and excellent storage facilities. The comfort of both patrons and players is assured through the use of both coal and oil furnaces, and the general lighting system is fitted for all requirements.

Responsible for Work

To Cecil Burgess goes the credit of being the architect of the remodelled structure, while Stewart Christie was the general contractor in charge of operations. Decorations were by George T. Green and the electrical installations were made by Stanley Lewis. Furnishings were provided by A.J. Freiman Limited and the windows were installed by the Colonial Art Glass Company. Materials were supplied by Murphy and Morrow and building hardware in many forms by W.A. Rankin, Limited. Equipment details were furnished and installed by W.G. Edge Limited. Electrical lighting and power is being furnished by the Ottawa Electric Company.

All features of the Little Theatre, new home of the Ottawa Drama League and centre of amateur dramatic art in the Capital, will be found very pleasing to all.[22]

The pride that members of the group—now numbering close to two thousand—felt in their theatre shines through in this piece, which one of the members prepared for the newspaper. It is no less evident in the report of the first production, which begins:

Last night, the Ottawa Drama League realized its dream when, before a capacity house in the beautiful new Little Theatre, St. John Ervine's new comedy "Anthony and Anna" was given its premiere showing here.

Fifteen years of planning and hoping culminated when the curtain rose at 8:30 o'clock and the theatre was introduced by a most appropriate prologue, written for the occasion by Duncan Campbell Scott and spoken by

22. *Ottawa Journal*, January 3, 1928, p. 14.

Prologue
By
Duncan Campbell Scott

Spoken
By
Dorothy White

At the opening of
The Little Theatre
OTTAWA

Fourth of January
1928

Dorothy White gave the first dramatic offering from the stage of the Ottawa Little Theatre before St. John Ervine's *Anthony and Anna* was presented on January 4, 1928.

Valentine Barrow models the dress that Dorothy White wore when she read the *Prologue*. (*Prologue* is reproduced in its entirety in Appendix III.)

Mrs. Louis White, better known to Ottawa audiences as Dorothy White.

At the end of the performance, as the final curtain was rung down, the audience of nearly 500 people broke into applause which must have amply repaid those who labored to bring the Ottawa Drama League to its present unique position. And among that audience of 500 people, not one word of dissatisfaction was heard.[23]

23. *Ottawa Journal*, January 5, 1928, p. 11.

It is not hard to imagine the excitement of every person who strolled through the foyer to take their seats in the auditorium of *their* theatre for that very first show. As Harley Granville-Barker wrote in his congratulatory letter when the new theatre opened: "Your theatre is founded on years of work and built of something better than bricks and mortar—a love of drama for its own sake. While that lives, how should it not prosper?" And prosper it did. Without doubt, the Ottawa Drama League was entering a new era.

Anthony and Anna by St. John Ervine was the first play presented in the Ottawa Drama League's own theatre, January 4, 1928.

CHAPTER 2

Reaching Out

A day will come when [they]...reach out their hands amid the stars.
H.G. Wells

The spirit of a nation, if it is to find full expression,
must include a National Drama.
Lord Bessborough[1]

"Theatre in Canada is dead." That warning from a friend in 1931 horrified Vere Brabazon Ponsonby, First Earl of Bessborough. He had just been appointed Governor General of Canada and had hoped that his deep love of theatre would be satisfied in his new home. At his Hampshire seat, Rowland's Castle in Stansted Park, he and his French actress wife had created the best-equipped private playhouse in England. Here, professional actors and directors presented plays for titled audiences—Lord Louis Mountbatten and his wife attended regularly, for instance. The London press frequently reviewed productions by the Stansted Players, which often included sets designed by Lord Bessborough or appearances by his son, Viscount Eric Duncannon.

Later, father and son were to design and act with Ottawa Little Theatre. Lord Bessborough's first set and Viscount Duncannon's first appearance on its stage took place shortly after they arrived in Canada, when the Montreal Repertory Theatre Players presented *The Cat and the Cherub* by C.B. Fernald. "This play," noted the program, "was produced last year in the Stansted Theatre by His Excellency the Earl of Bessborough, who has designed the set for the present production."

1. From his message in the first Dominion Drama Festival program, April 24, 1933.

Described in the *Ottawa Journal* report of the opening on December 16, 1931 as "a picturesque though not very vital little melodrama," the big news about the evening was that "one of the largest and most distinguished first night audiences ever to attend a Little theater *[sic]* opening went to the Drama League's miniature playhouse on King Edward Avenue last night. The chief reason for this was that it was a sort of gala occasion. Besides a three-act comedy (A.A. Milne's *The Truth About Blayds*)[2] by members of the Drama League—the customary fare—there was also on the bill a one-act play presented by the Montreal Repertory Players. In addition, Their Excellencies the Governor General and Lady Bessborough were among those present to witness the first public stage performance of their son, Lord Duncannon, an amateur player of no mean ability, who took one of the leading parts in the curtain-raiser. The proceedings, we are happy to report, went off beautifully."

Despite this early theatrical highlight when the new Governor General arrived in Ottawa in 1931, his first reaction was that "the theatre habit had died. Theatres taken over by film companies left few places available for people to rent…the world depression had practically killed touring by professional companies, either from England or from France."[3]

However, Lord Bessborough soon discovered that the end of touring by such stage greats as Sarah Bernhardt and Sir Henry Irving had not ended theatre in Canada. Rather, it had signalled a new beginning. "Instinctively...in centres thousands of miles removed from one another, [Canadians] laid the foundations of a people's theatre....I learnt that literally hundreds of drama leagues were in active operation all over Canada, some (like Ottawa Little Theatre) already possessing their own little theatres."[4]

Lord Bessborough soon became a regular Ottawa Little Theatre patron and invited members of the Ottawa Drama League executive to Rideau Hall to discuss the state of theatre in the Dominion. Then, a letter from Lillian Myers of the Saskatoon Little Theatre, recommending the founding of a Canadian Drama League, prompted the Governor General to set his great idea in motion.

"Why not harness and consolidate this national movement by holding a Dominion Drama Festival?"[5] he said in October 1932. Why not? Lord Bessborough

2. The Ottawa Drama League took this production to Moyse Hall in Montreal after its Ottawa run ended.
3. From a speech by the Earl of Bessborough, reprinted in *The Curtain Call*, Vol. 7, December 1935, p. 3, from the *London Morning Post.*
4. *Ibid.*
5. *Ibid.*

prepared to write to "lieutenant governors of the provinces, principals of universities, directors of little theatres and representatives of the boy scouts and girl guides announcing his interest in organizing a festival that would create national interest and be of educational value."[6] He promoted the cause at every opportunity:

> *I should like to see as a normal part of our life in this country, dramatic performances taking place of plays by Canadian authors and music by Canadian composers, with scenic decoration and costumes by Canadian artists, performed by Canadian players. The drama can be made not only an artistic but a great educational influence. I visualize a movement that might develop into a great Drama League, Dominion wide. The keen and growing interest in the little theatre and repertory theatre movement, extending as it does right across the Dominion from Ottawa, through Winnipeg and Vancouver, is proof in my mind that a movement for national drama might be born.*[7]

And born it was, with Lord Bessborough as its patron, former Prime Minister Sir Robert Borden its first president and Vincent Massey its chairman. Colonel Henry Osborne of the Ottawa Drama League's board of directors was named vice-chairman and honorary director. Nationwide support for the festival was assured by the appointment of lieutenant-governors, federal politicians, provincial premiers, education ministers, university heads, church leaders and presidents of theatre groups to a general festival committee. "The dignity and prestige of the Little Theatre movement are immensely enhanced by this tremendous endorsation," commented a report in the October 29, 1932 issue of the *Globe*.[8]

The endorsement spilled over to the Ottawa Drama League; its recently acquired theatre was to be the home of the Dominion Drama Festival for its first five years. Lord Bessborough was both patron of the Festival and honorary president of the Ottawa Drama League. So was the next Governor General, Lord Tweedsmuir,[9] who soon after his appointment, gave "tangible evidence of [his] interest in the amateur stage by attending a performance of the Ottawa Drama League. The Government House party...was present at the production of *Escape* by John Galsworthy....At the

6. Quoted in *Love and Whisky* by Betty Lee, McClelland and Stewart Ltd., 1973, *op. cit.*, p. 87.
7. From a speech to the Empire Club in Toronto, November 1932, quoted in *Love and Whisky*, *op. cit.*, p. 88.
8. *Ibid.*, p. 98.
9. Author John Buchan.

conclusion of the offering [they] made a tour back-stage to inspect the equipment of Ottawa's excellent Little Theatre. Warm congratulations were offered the cast and the director, Mrs. Dorothy White, for having given a smartly paced and beautifully staged performance of a play worthy of the best efforts of one of the Dominion's most advanced Little Theatre groups."[10]

The theatre maintained its connection with Rideau Hall, as Rica McLean Farquharson wrote in 1941. "The Governor General, Earl of Athlone, and Princess Alice continue the tradition, since the time of Lord Bessborough, whereby the current Governor General is Honorary President of the Ottawa Drama League, Their position is not only an 'honorary' one. They attend and enjoy plays."[11] The tradition lives on. Today's programs continue to bear the name of the current Governor General as honorary patron.

In April, 1933, "the impact of the first DDF Final on Canada's capital was enormous. Theatre was the current vogue because of Bessborough's fascinated involvement, so the Ottawa Little Theatre was packed for all occasions....Prominent citizens...decided that if the...Governor General, the Prime Minister, Vincent Massey and other notables were backing the DDF, they would outdo themselves to make the week a glittering occasion. Society writers fought to spread the news."[12] Theatre groups came from far and wide to compete for the coveted Bessborough Trophy, to be presented by the Governor General himself on the stage of the Ottawa Little Theatre.

The Earl of Bessborough, the Governor General who founded the Dominion Drama Festival in 1933, donated the festival's top award: The Bessborough Trophy.

Ottawa Little Theatre stalwart Dorothy White—by this time also a member of the local Dominion Drama Festival committee and, later, to be its president—headed the group greeting the visiting drama troupes and

10. "Ottawa Little Theatre Honoured," *The Curtain Call*, Vol. 7, No. 3, December 1935, p. 1.
11. "International Seasoning of Ottawa Little Theatre" by Rica McLean Farquharson in *The Curtain Call*, Vol. 12, No. 8, May-June 1941, p. 3.
12. *Ibid.*, p. 114.

carrying them off to the members' homes where they were billeted for the duration of the festival. "Long after the awards have been made and the excitement...has subsided...the sincerity of her welcome is remembered gratefully by players from all parts of Canada who came to the capital strangers and found there friends."[13]

> *From the [train] station, each drama group was escorted triumphantly to the Ottawa Little Theatre, registered and presented with a silver pin bearing the Bessborough arms and decorated with the blue and red Bessborough colours. Local journalists—happily aware that the Little Theatre was one of the best equipped in Canada...— hovered, pencils poised, to record the comments of visitors from the boondocks when they glimpsed the place for the first time.*[14]

Ottawa Little Theatre remained the home of the Dominion Drama Festival until 1938. During those years, as the festival grew in importance, the trip to the theatrical Mecca became the highlight of the year for drama groups across Canada. Even after the Festival left the capital to move around the country, the prestige of being its first home lingered. Similarly, the close connection with a Governor General so passionately committed to the theatre added to Ottawa Little Theatre's special aura.

Not that the relationship with the Earl of Bessborough was completely smooth. In 1932, he sponsored and designed the sets for a production of *Hamlet*—with his 19-year-old son in the lead. Even if this caused only a minor ripple of awkwardness at the theatre, a spat between the young Lord Duncannon and his leading lady in the next season's production of *Romeo and Juliet* (with sets also designed by Lord Bessborough) caused a greater problem. Romeo swore at Juliet (played by Ottawa Drama League member Julia MacBrien) during rehearsals and her father threatened to avenge the insult by rearranging the young Viscount's handsome features.

But the difficulty soon passed and the cachet of the close connection with Rideau Hall remained. The *Ottawa Journal* review of the production on December 26, 1933 began by noting that "Lord Duncannon, elder son of the Governor General and Countess of Bessborough, and other members of the cast of the Ottawa Drama League presentation of Shakespeare's *Romeo and Juliet* again delighted an audience which filled the Little Theater *[sic]* to capacity....Once again the Governor

13. *The Curtain Call*, Vol. 6, No. 7, April 1935, p. 3.
14. *Love and Whisky, op. cit.*, p. 115.

General and the Countess of Bessborough were present to see their son, who gave an interpretation of the role of Romeo,[15] and able supporting members of the cast show histrionic brilliancy. Rt. Hon. W.L. Mackenzie King was a member of the vice-regal party."

ABOVE: Julia MacBrien (later Murphy) played Juliet opposite Viscount Eric Duncannon's Romeo in 1933.

LEFT: Viscount Eric Duncannon, the son of the Earl of Bessborough, played the title role in the Montreal Repertory Theatre/Ottawa Drama league production of *Hamlet* in 1932. He was 19 years old. His father designed the sets.

"Ottawa Little Theatre was a special part of Ottawa society at that time," recalls Wallis White, son of Dorothy White. And continued to be so after the outbreak of World War II, noted Rica Farquharson in 1941. "The Princess Juliana of the

15. From the perspective of the present, the careful reference to Lord Duncannon's performance suggests it was considered politic to avoid negative comment about the quality of his acting.

Netherlands seldom misses a play....She discusses her reactions in animated tones. She has season tickets for the Drama League productions and arrives unobtrusively with her party. Among the diplomatic corps who have tickets for the season are representatives of the Polish, Belgium, Dutch and American legations. The decorative Mrs. C.Y. Shih and her husband, Consul-General for China, are also familiar figures in the foyer. Count Podoski, Consul-General of Poland, gave an interesting talk to the Workshop during the season. He attends the plays and is an authority on the theatre. Members of the legations in Ottawa are referred to as the most charming and tolerant members of Little Theatre audiences."[16]

"Before the war, if you came to a show down here, you wore a black tie. I've even seen people here with opera capes. But when Bessborough came, he always came backstage. They used to telephone and say, 'Can you find a spot backstage for the Governor-General to hang his coat?'" Bill Adkins, Ottawa Little Theatre's long-time stage manager, told the *Ottawa Citizen* as he looked back after 45 years in the job.[17]

Unquestionably, it was Lord Bessborough's patronage of both the Ottawa Little Theatre and the Dominion Drama Festival that brought the theatre nationwide recognition and admiration. Early on, one admirer noted that "the Drama League is entitled to public thanks for its continued good work in providing civilized plays in a veritable dramatic wilderness."[18] Accolades for the theatre were often incorporated in post-festival assessments; for instance, "...the Little Theatre at Ottawa in which the Festival has taken place these past three years...fills too important a place in the entertainment of the community to permit its doors to be closed for any length of time," noted *The Curtain Call* in 1935. "As for dust—perish the thought! Its board of management is much too efficient to allow the existence of the smallest particle of dust, as they will testify who throughout Festival week climbed the high ledge at the back of the house (where dust might reasonably be expected to lurk) and perched there like a row of birds of rare plumage when seats were not available on the floor below....a pleasant calm now pervades...the scene of the contest...and...nothing but satisfaction is expressed for the manner in which the Festival was conducted and the awards were made."[19]

"These early festivals did a great deal for the [Ottawa Little] Theatre, not only by

16. "International Seasoning of Ottawa Little Theatre," *op. cit.*, pp. 3-4.
17. From an interview by Audrey Ashley, *Ottawa Citizen*, January 27, 1968.
18. Unsigned note in Ottawa Little Theatre scrapbook (1928-1940)
19. *The Curtain Call*, Vol. 6, No. 8, May 1935, p. 1.

giving the active membership new goals to aim at, but also by providing our audience with an opportunity of listening to some of the foremost theatrical authorities of the English-speaking stage, explaining the fundamentals of good acting and direction and in so doing opening new vistas of theatrical enjoyment," wrote Michael Meiklejohn, then president of the theatre group, in 1957.[20]

Together, the Dominion Drama Festival and Ottawa Drama League (renamed Ottawa Little Theatre in 1951) did a great deal for the growth of Canadian drama. Even at the inaugural Festival, Colonel Henry Osborne announced that a $100 award would be offered to the "author of the best Canadian play, considered as a dramatic composition, presented in the Festival of 1934."[21] British director Rupert Harvey, in Ottawa to direct Ottawa Drama League's *Romeo and Juliet* (the production infamous for the altercation with Viscount Duncannon), and to speak during the Dominion Drama Festival, was anxious to see plays by Canadian writers. "I am particularly keen on fostering the work of Canadian dramatists and hope to find a large percentage of plays by Canadian authors among the entrants," he wrote in 1933.[22]

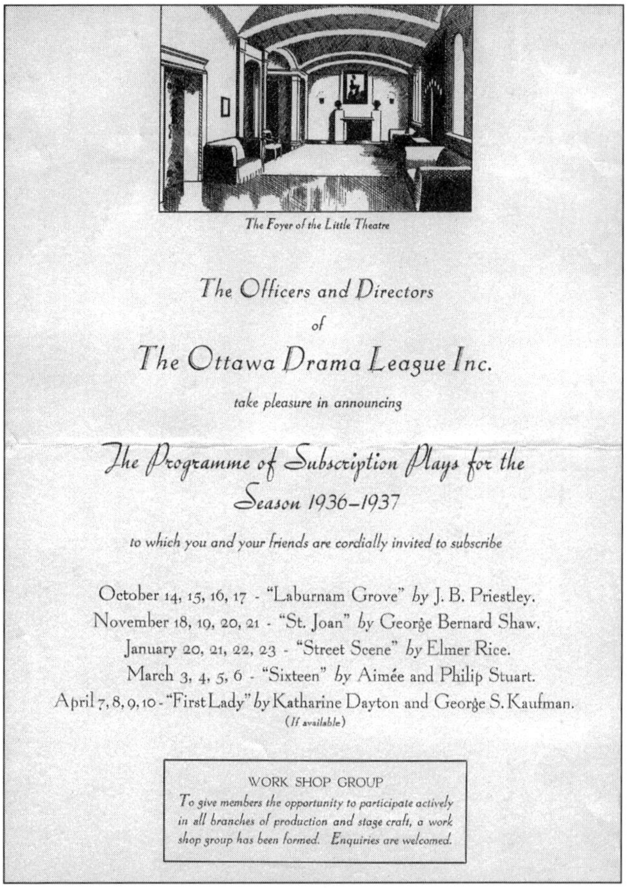

The Foyer of the Little Theatre

The Officers and Directors

of

The Ottawa Drama League Inc.

take pleasure in announcing

The Programme of Subscription Plays for the Season 1936–1937

to which you and your friends are cordially invited to subscribe

October 14, 15, 16, 17 - "Laburnam Grove" *by* J. B. Priestley.
November 18, 19, 20, 21 - "St. Joan" *by* George Bernard Shaw.
January 20, 21, 22, 23 - "Street Scene" *by* Elmer Rice.
March 3, 4, 5, 6 - "Sixteen" *by* Aimée and Philip Stuart.
April 7, 8, 9, 10 - "First Lady" *by* Katharine Dayton and George S. Kaufman.
(*If available*)

WORK SHOP GROUP
To give members the opportunity to participate actively in all branches of production and stage craft, a work shop group has been formed. Enquiries are welcomed.

As part of the drive to encourage new plays, the Ottawa Drama League founded its Workshop in 1936. This experimental group, begun by three members—Michael Meiklejohn, Julia (MacBrien) Murphy and Eric Stangroom—was "dedicated to the proposition that theatres thrive if all the members can participate some of the time,

20. *Ottawa Little Theatre Newsletter*, Vol. 2, No. 4, January 1957, p. 1.
21. *The Curtain Call*, Vol. 5, No. 3, December 1933, p. 2.
22. *Ibid.*, p. 1.

rather than some of the members all of the time" and ensured that it "presented original and experimental plays, made room for inexperienced people to participate, and permitted old members to try a hand at new things."[23] Workshop plays were presented on Sunday evenings for more than twenty years. Admission was free, because the main aim was to give "would-be actors, writers, stagehands, directors, and all the 'stage-struck' (a chance) to satisfy yearnings for active participation in the theatre."[24]

For a while, the League ran a Radio Class in conjunction with the Workshop. In 1941 "amateur dramatic circles in Ottawa (were) again in the lead with something new and revolutionary in Canada. Working hand-in-hand with the Little Theatre movement and the Workshop Group of the Ottawa Drama League, members of the newly formed Radio Class, are tackling radio in the same light as dramatics, applying a 'stage approach to radio'."[25] Renovation of the studios of Ottawa's Canadian Broadcasting Corporation (CBC) radio station, located in the Château Laurier Hotel (where they are still situated) had been completed. It was now possible to produce radio drama here. First, however, CBC producer Bob Edmunds was determined to build a coterie of radio actors.

> *When Ottawa woke to find that she now happily had the facilities she yearned for, the talent file, kept to assist in casting problems, was found to be as bare as old Mother Hubbard's cupboard, as far as trained actors were concerned....to cope with this problem, the idea of training—right from the bottom of the ladder of technique—a sufficient number of persons to form the nucleus of a talent file, made the establishment of radio classes a necessity. The logical place to look for persons interested in these classes was the Ottawa Drama League....The classes, which are already in progress, will cover all the fields of radio for good grounding....Upon these classes depend whether Ottawa will make its name in radio dramatic circles....It is to be hoped these classes will be the beginning of another successful page in Ottawa's amateur acting history, and equal to her past triumphs.*[26]

The radio classes were a short-term venture, apparently stopped after having served

23. *Ottawa Little Theatre Newsletter*, Vol. 2, No. 1, September 1956, p. 3.
24. *Ibid.*
25. "Ottawa's Radio Classes" by William Freeman, *The Curtain Call*, Vol. 12, No. 6, March 1941, p. 2.
26. *Ibid.*

their avowed purpose of training local actors in radio techniques. The Workshop, too, was eventually discontinued when the increase in the number of mainstage productions meant that there was neither time nor space to accommodate a second stage; but even after the Workshop's demise, its legacy remained. "The most lasting contribution of the workshop, and its most important,...was the annual play-writing contest....We always produced three top winners, and that was how in 1947 I came to direct Robertson Davies' *Overlaid*," writes actress Amelia Hall. (Amelia Hall was the first Canadian and the first woman to speak on the Stratford stage. Internationally acclaimed author Robertson Davies was a multiple-winner and later a judge of the Ottawa Little Theatre One-Act Playwriting Competition.)[27] In 1949, she was in the cast of the Ottawa Drama League production of Robertson Davies' *Eros at Breakfast*, directed by Michael Meiklejohn, which represented Canada at the Edinburgh Festival. "That did Canadian theatre a lot of good because it made them realize there was such a thing," recalls Mr. Meiklejohn's widow, Barbara.

Florence Fancott and Claude Jutras appearing in *Night of Storm* by Norman Williams, one of the winners of the 1954 One-Act Playwriting Competition. The competition award included a production, while the Workshop was in existence. *PHOTO: VAN*

27. *Life Before Stratford* by Amelia Hall, Dundurn Press, Toronto, 1989, p. 49.

The national playwriting competition remains an annual event. Winning plays still receive cash awards, though without the Workshop, they are no longer guaranteed a production.

Another legacy of the early years was the children's theatre. "When we first came to Ottawa (in 1954), people talked constantly about the wonderful children's theatre productions that Julia Murphy and Marian Taylor put on," says current theatre president Sybil Cooke. "As far as I can remember," laughs Mrs. Meiklejohn, "Michael, Julia Murphy and Marian Taylor set up the theatre for children. Then he turned round and said, 'now you run it'." Then a drama and speech teacher, as well as a member of the cast of many of the plays at Ottawa Little Theatre, this is just what Barbara Meiklejohn did. Sponsored by the larger theatre, the children's theatre's highly acclaimed productions toured local schools, and a school of the theatre soon developed as a natural offshoot of the theatre for children. By the time Ottawa Little Theatre member Bill Glenn, now a Hollywood producer, took over the classes in 1956, they, like the mainstage theatre productions, were extremely popular. "Bill Glenn's various theatre classes are now full to capacity and a waiting list is being kept," announced the January 1957 issue of *Ottawa Little Theatre Newsletter*. The theatre classes, for adults as well as children, continue, now with a summer camp added to the list of "voice, movement, improv and scene reading for juniors (9-11 years), intermediates (12-14 years) and seniors (15-18 years)." Adult drama classes, started in 1976, promise "to introduce adults to the basic discipline and techniques of an actor's craft" and give more experienced actors greater "focus on characterization and script analysis."[28]

"I vividly remember the first time we put on an adult class," recalls Leonie Gardner, who originated the adult classes and is still teaching at Ottawa Little Theatre. "When I arrived to register students, there was a line-up from the front door of the theatre all the way down Besserer Street. Obviously, there was a niche to be filled there. At that time, you see, there weren't any other classes like it in Ottawa." Today, more than twenty years later, both adult and youth classes remain a popular part of Ottawa Little Theatre's annual calendar, another of the threads that binds past and future in its theatrical history.

---

28. Advertisements for summer drama classes in February 7 and June 20, 1987 issues of the *Ottawa Citizen*.

CHAPTER 3

The Magic of the Stage

...What we now see
Came from a seed planted courageously
...to enhance
The Joy of Life by the Drama[1]

"The Ottawa Drama League's new playhouse on King Edward Avenue will be the center *[sic]* of theatrical experiment in the Capital and it may also be the only place where serious plays will be available for the growing number of persons who are taking an intelligent interest in the drama as an art as well as a form of entertainment," announced a 1929 subscription appeal. "The enterprise of the Drama League in the matter is to be commended. The best way to express appreciation is to join the League and so become a subscribing seatholder at the new Little Theater *[sic]*. Already there are more members in the Ottawa Drama League than any other similar organization in Canada."[2]

For a number of years, Ottawa responded enthusiastically to the call to support its theatre. The Russell Theatre had closed and the city had no other major playhouse. Ottawa Little Theatre, particularly because of its close connection with the Dominion Drama Festival, was both the city's dramatic heart and its social centre. Membership grew steadily each year. Ottawa Little Theatre was definitely *the* place to go to see "plays as various as life...dramas where the overtones of life are blent."[3] "The 500-seat theatre flourished. The Ottawa Drama League shared the

1. From the *Prologue* by Duncan Campbell Scott, presented at the opening of the theatre on January 4, 1928. The *Prologue* is reproduced in its entirety in Appendix III of this book.
2. Ottawa Little Theatre scrapbook, No. 4.
3. *Prologue* by Duncan Campbell Scott, *op. cit.*

stage with professional groups who would rent it during their visits to town."[4] Such famous actors as Tyrone Guthrie, Ruth Draper and Donald Wolfit were among those to appear at Ottawa Little Theatre. Even before the group had its own building, it had shared a stage with some great names, recalled Elizabeth Cruikshank:

> *One time, Sarah Bernhardt, on one...of her farewell tours, was coming to the Russell Theatre. A group of us really worked hard to clean up a filthy dressing room for her, and someone managed to borrow a tri-color, which we draped carefully in the room. The next day we went back to get the flag and found that, without saying anything, she had packed it in her trunk and taken it away with her.*[5]

The minor flurry occasioned by the flag was no more than a momentary ripple in the development of the theatre, however. "The Little Theatre...proved a boon to Ottawa...frequently used by other amateur organizations for dramatic and musical performances, and it has provided a place where many eminent professionals might be heard and seen, who would otherwise have scarcely been able to appear in Ottawa at all....There has hardly been a week during the whole season when some entertainment was not being given there."[6]

Unquestionably, Ottawa Little Theatre was well established as the centre of drama in the capital and the focal point of the Dominion Drama Festival. Then the Festival's "National Committee decided to make [the festival] a movable feast and to accept Winnipeg's invitation for 1938."[7]

A year later, World War II broke out and the festival was suspended for the duration of the war. In Ottawa, as around the world, theatre took a back seat to the war effort. "The only way we stayed alive was from rentals," recalled stage manager Bill Adkins looking back on forty-five years as stage manager. (He actually held the job for close to sixty years until ill-health forced retirement on him shortly before his death at age 93.) "From 1940 to 1947 the theatre was rented for movies, but even then we did a show a month. All the downstairs was kept clear. From midnight Saturday until 12 o'clock on Sunday we'd take down all the movie equipment and start putting up the set."[8]

4. From an interview with Sheila McCook, *Ottawa Citizen*, August 6, 1969, *op. cit.*
5. *Ibid.*
6. *The Canadian Forum*, Vol. 10, May 1930, p. 306.
7. "Drama Festival Leaves Ottawa" by Hector Charlesworth, *Saturday Night*, Vol. 52, May 8, 1937, p. 12. From 1938 until its demise in 1978, the festival (renamed Theatre Canada in 1970) rotated around Canada.
8. From a profile by Audrey Ashley, *Ottawa Citizen*, January 27, 1968.

Bea Whitfield, Bea Brace, Jack Little and Barbara Meiklejohn in the 1947 production of *Uncle Harry* by Thomas Job, directed by Amelia Hall. *PHOTO: VINCENT THOMAS*

The theatre "was saved from closing its doors by renting the [building] out as a motion picture house. Under the arrangement, the League had the use of the basement at all times, the entire theatre every Sunday and five complete weeks during the season for its own plays," notes the introduction of the theatre's 75th anniversary cookbook. "The war years were years of frustration and discomfort—cramped rehearsal space, difficulties with scenery building and friction with the tenants....Despite the tensions, the League performed its plays for the military personnel stationed in the district and contributed regularly from its receipts to the Red Cross and various wartime funds."[9]

In spite of all the problems, membership grew as the war effort brought newcomers to Ottawa. Members included:

9. During this period, some changes were made to the building, writes Valentine Barrow in "The Ottawa Little Theatre: a Brief History," a paper for the University of Victoria, April 3, 1984: "The building was modified in the early 1940s by the enlargement of the main entrance and the addition, at the east end of the auditorium, of an approximately twelve-foot wide office with projection room above. These alterations were made because the theatre was rented during the war years for the showing of art films." *Theatre Cook Book*, Ottawa Little Theatre, 1988, coordinated by Bea Brace, p. iv.

> *...men in khaki, blue, navy; men in Ottawa without their families; young wives with husbands in the Air Force; dollar-a-year men, guests from the Old Land; youthful brides and grooms transferred to the Capital; stenographers starting in the Civil Service; boys and girls who have never before seen legitimate drama—all these and hundreds more—pour into the doors of the playhouse that was once a church....Fervently, loyally, in the face of tremendous war activity and responsibilities, the Capital of Canada is proclaiming: 'The play must go on!'*[10]
>
> *Casting was not easy. Many former actors had joined the army, navy, air force or were on war jobs that made attendance at rehearsals impossible, but...players appeared from all over the world. They arrived at the playhouse to say they were living in Ottawa now. They had been in amateur or professional drama circles in England or the United States, Portugal, Spain, Cairo. From the Seven Seas they came. Could they have parts in a play?*[11]

One such hopeful was a young American who stood in the wings awaiting her turn to audition for a part in the next play. "The comedy called for a shriek backstage. 'Can you shriek?' asked Ruth (Burkholder née Ruggles, the director). 'I did it for Orson Welles,' was the answer. And so Polly Smiley Ayer, once a member of Orson Welles' Mercury Theatre of the Air and former Ted Shawn dancer, began an active winter at the Ottawa Little Theatre while her husband was overseas with the RAF."[12]

"There were still some very good shows then," recalls Wallis White. "During the war, they put on a fabulous review directed by Saul Rae, I remember, a wonderful show. And, of course, just before the war there was (Terence Rattigan's) *French Without Tears*." This award-winning production, in which Mr. White, then 12 years old, played the part of young Lord Heybrook, was directed by Mr. White's mother, Dorothy. It was the big winner at the 1938 Dominion Drama Festival, carrying off the prized Bessborough Trophy.

By 1947, the Ottawa Drama League was able to reclaim its theatre and return to the rhythm of mounting a regular season of plays. For many, it was akin to a homecoming to a special place. Robert MacNeil, author of *Wordstruck*, recalls how, as a teenager, he hid "in the magical darkness backstage at the Ottawa Little Theatre, to be a stagehand or extra prop man or scene painter—anything, the most menial task,

10. "International Seasoning of Ottawa Little Theatre," *op. cit.*, p. 4.
11. *Ibid.*, p. 3.
12. *Ibid.*

that permitted me to breathe that charmed air....Others who have been stage-struck will recognise an acute and hopeless case. It was like being in love. I rushed breathlessly, dropping anything to be there....I was infatuated with the ambiance....The very air in the green room, a certain musty perfume coming from old make-up and cosÙumes faintly redolent of the bodies that had worn them, that very air was sexy in an abstract way. It took me a while to realise that I was not the only one who felt it. Even the older people who had been coming for years arrived with a little extra juice that did not flow in their lives outside the theatre."[13]

That was certainly true for Florence Fancott. Fresh from England in 1949, she had acted with the Northampton Repertory Company, shared a stage with Errol Flynn and dressed Sybil Thorndike's hair. "I loved the theatre," she says. "As soon as (husband) Ted and I arrived in Ottawa and heard that there was a theatre, I wanted to join. I went to the Workshop tea (part of the annual membership drive) and said that I was willing to do anything."

She was assigned to do the props for the next production, *The Two Mrs. Carrolls* by Martin Vale. "I had never done props before, but I didn't care. I just wanted to be part of it, to be in that theatre," she says. "The theatre! I couldn't believe that this was an amateur theatre. In England, we'd acted in draughty, old halls."

As it turned out, she did not work on props for *The Two Mrs. Carrolls* or any other show at Ottawa Little Theatre. Instead, she was asked to play the lead in that production and many, many more over the next thirty-five years.

Florence Fancott in the 1956 production of *The Women* by Clare Booth Luce, directed by Floyd Caza.

PHOTO: VAN

"People used to come especially to see Flo and Roy Hayden-Hinsley," says Sybil Cooke, who has been an

13. From *Wordstruck* by Robert MacNeil. Copyright (c) 1989 by Neely Productions, Ltd. Used by permission of Viking Penguin, a division of Penguin Books USA Inc., p. 137.

Ottawa Little Theatre member since 1954 and president since 1990. "They were a magical duo to watch."

The magic of the theatre touched many. Ottawa Little Theatre might be the doorway to a career as a professional actor—it was for Dan Aykroyd, Rich Little and William Shatner, for instance—or it might be the catalyst for a journey down a different road. It certainly changed the life of one young Armenian immigrant. In 1932, he was a newcomer to Ottawa, employed as an assistant to John Powis of the Powis Photographic Studio.

"One day in October, 1932," he writes in his memoir,[14] "I met a young man...who said to me, 'I am going to the theatre tonight; would you like to come along?'...I was not too strongly impressed by the play (which, being in English, I had still some difficulty in following) but I was very much struck by the timbre of the voice of the leading lady, for I have always been extremely sensitive to voices."

That young actress was Solange Gauthier, one of the leading lights of Ottawa Little Theatre at the time. "After the performance, my new friend led me backstage and down to a dressing-room which he entered without knocking the door," continues the memoir. "There reclined an attractive young woman, with one foot pointed towards the ceiling as she pulled on a stocking. She threw a gay smile at [us] and shouted...'Well, if you will come into my dressing-room when I'm pulling on my stockings'—and went right ahead with the other one. She said afterwards that she thought it took me several years to get over the shock of our first meeting, but it was not so; I thought she was wonderful, then as always."

So wonderful, in fact, that he was to marry her. He was also to become one of the world's most famous photographers. The young man was Yousuf Karsh.

Solange brought me into association with the Little Theatre movement in Ottawa, and it was largely through this connection that I started on my present career. I photographed Solange as an actress, and I watched Solange directing plays. As instructions about lighting effects were given by the directors, a new world opened to me. This experience of photographing actors on the stage, with stage lighting, was electrifying. Garo[15] *had taught me to work with daylight, where one had to wait for the lighting to be right. In this new situation the director could command the lighting to do what he wished. The*

14. *In Search of Greatness: Reflections of Yousuf Karsh*, University of Toronto Press, 1962, p. 42.
15. Photographer John H. Garo of Boston.

Solange Gauthier and William Brodie in the 1933 production of *And So to Bed* by J.B. Fagan, directed by William Cromarty. PHOTO: KARSH

This study of Solange (Gauthier) Karsh dancing under a willow was used in the design of the top award in Ottawa Little Theatre's One-Act Playwriting Competition. PHOTO: KARSH

> *unlimited possibilities of artificial lighting overwhelmed me. Mood effects could be created, selected, modified, intensified. I was thrilled by the realization of this new method of interpreting life, this new means of expression.*[16]

Karsh's special interest in theatrical photography and his particular relationship with Ottawa Little Theatre led to his appointment as official photographer for the first Dominion Drama Festival in 1933. Later that year, Karsh photographed Lord Duncannon and Julia MacBrien in the Ottawa Little Theatre production of *Romeo and Juliet*. The photographs covered a full page in *Saturday Night*, a happy event that "may have had something to do with...the social prominence of the actors...as well as the art of the photographer," writes Karsh modestly.[17] In any case, it marked the beginning of his friendship with Viscount Duncannon, who asked his parents to

16. *In Search of Greatness* by Yousuf Karsh, *op. cit.*, p. 48.
17. *Ibid.*, p. 49.

sit for Karsh. The Bessborough photographs were an artistic success and a passport to a career of portraits of famous figures. And it all began at Ottawa Little Theatre, which still proudly displays a selection of Karsh's early theatrical photographs. He even appears on the other side of the camera occasionally, having obliged Solange by taking a small part now and then.[18] When she died in 1961, he continued to support the theatre by establishing the Solange Karsh Award in her name. It remains the top prize offered in Ottawa Little Theatre's One-Act Playwriting Competition.[19]

George Browne in the 1936 production of Merton Hodge's *The Wind and the Rain*, directed by Dorothy White. PHOTO: KARSH

Many audience members support the theatre as strongly as Karsh in their own ways, particularly when they feel a newspaper critic has spoken too harshly. In 1947, for instance, a Miss M.D.M. could not let the *Ottawa Journal*'s negative review of *The Great Big Doorstep* by Frances Goodrich and Albert Hackett pass without comment:

May I be permitted a little space in your valuable paper to let you and others know that I heartily disagree with B.W.'s criticism in The Journal of the first offering of the Ottawa Drama League (this season). I for one, and several others who I have talked with, enjoyed it very much. It was a good clean

18. He took the part of "A Small Chess Player" in *See Naples and Die* by Elmer Rice in March 1934, for example. Although he did not have a speaking part, he apparently amused the chess players in the audience, by making assorted wrong moves.
19. The other two awards, named after Dorothy White and the University Women's Club of Ottawa, are further reminders of the theatre's heritage.

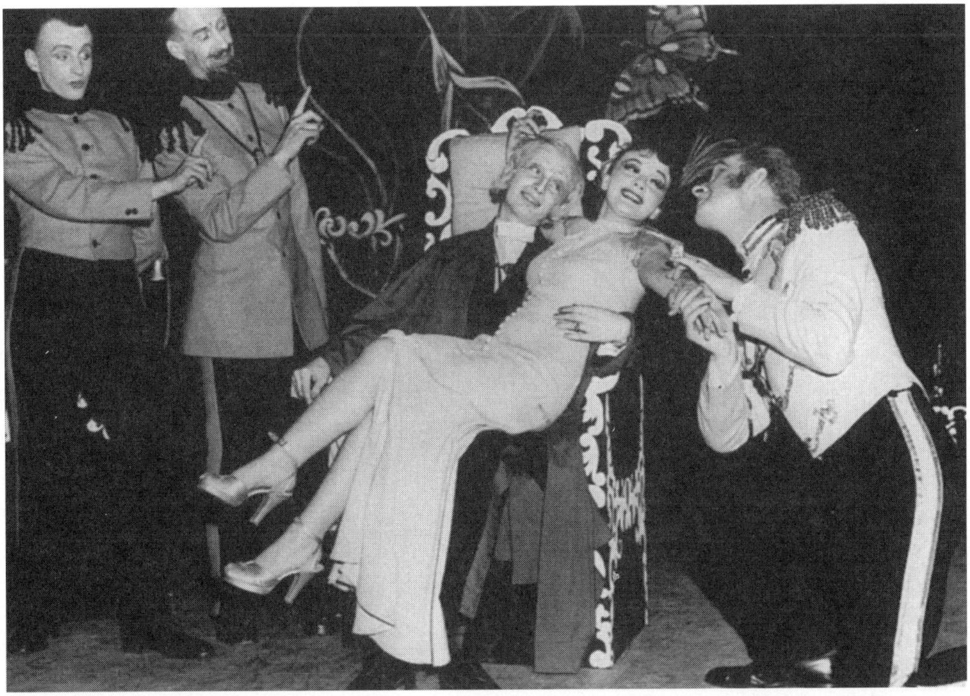

In 1949, the Ottawa Drama League took their production of the winner of that year's one-act playwriting competition to the Edinburgh Festival. The play, directed by Michael Meiklejohn, was *Eros at Breakfast* by Robertson Davies. Amelia Hall was in the cast.

play, and the characters in it were quite real....I consider the choice of play was a very good one.[20]

Letters like this are a reminder of how strongly the audiences felt about their theatre. *Plus ça change, plus c'est la même chose.* Similar letters are still being written.

Ottawa Little Theatre occupies a special place in the hearts of many, who, year after year, come from near and far to take their seats (the same seats each season). One of these is Mary Gallagher of Alexandria, more than one hundred kilometres from Ottawa. Still a season-ticket holder after well over half a century, she has been a regular Ottawa Little Theatre patron since her high school days in the 1920s.

20. Letter to the Editor of the *Ottawa Journal*, November 6, 1947. The offending portion of the review, published November 5, had commented: "The choice of play was unfortunate. A competent cast struggled valiantly but, for the most part, stilted and stereotyped lines hindered them from wringing humour and pathos from the supposed comedy....the pace was too slow, the situations and conversations too unbelievable—mainly the fault of the play itself—for a good performance."

Julia (MacBrien) Murphy in a private production of *Blood Wedding* by Garcia Lorca in 1954 by The Saturday Players (previously the Junior Theatre section of Ottawa Little Theatre).
PHOTO: VAN

"I began going with my family when we lived in Ottawa," she says. "I remember it was a very fussy place then. So many of the women wore evening clothes and even the man who took the tickets wore a tuxedo. Then we moved to Montreal, so I didn't go as much for a while, but it was definitely going to Ottawa Little Theatre that started my love of theatre. There was a time when I used to go off to New York at the drop of a hat and I think some of the plays at Ottawa Little Theatre are as good as the shows I saw in New York. I don't go there much any more but I still come to Ottawa Little Theatre on the last Saturday of each play. I wouldn't miss it."

No more would many of Ottawa Little Theatre's long-time patrons, who believe, as Solange Karsh once said, that "theatre is such a civilized thing." Arthur Davison, president of Ottawa Little Theatre in 1954, voiced a similar thought when he spoke of theatre as "an event to anticipate and reflect on [that] enlivens the body and spirit."[21] The magic of the theatre continues to call to performers and patrons.

21. Note from the President's Page in the Ottawa Little Theatre program for *The Moon in the Yellow River* by Denis Johnston, December 6-11, 1954.

CHAPTER 4

Changing With the Times—a Little

...to change what we can; to better what we can
Robert Louis Stevenson

With its traditions set and its position as an integral part of the city's cultural fabric well established, the Ottawa Drama League had reached a developmental plateau, even a slight downward turn. It began its fortieth season with a new name, a first step in responding to a drop in membership—from 2,000 to 1,600. Now officially known as Ottawa Little Theatre—"a name more in keeping with the practice of other amateur groups in Canada,"[1] the change acknowledged that the theatre "needed new vigor"[2] and could not rest on the laurels of past glory.

By this time, the city had a professional theatre group, the Canadian Repertory Theatre,[3] which meant that Ottawa Little Theatre was no longer the only theatrical act in town. "For some time we have had keen competition for our share of the theatre patron's leisure hours and loose change," wrote Arthur Davison, then president, in 1954. "We have kept abreast of this. Now comes the ever-increasing challenge of TV which purveys entertainment in the large economy size every night of the week."[4]

Arthur Davison wrote in a program note that "a strong membership is the best foundation on which to build our theatrical structure....(Members) have provided a certain stability on which we may lean without fear of being let down....We look on our Theatre as something more than a purveyor of entertainment. We strive to cre-

1. *Theatre Cook Book, op. cit.*, p. iv.
2. "New Name: New Impetus" by Margaret Ness, *Saturday Night*, December 15, 1951, p. 73.
3. Incorporated in 1950.
4. Note in program of *The Moon in the Yellow River* by Denis Johnston, December 6-11, 1954.

Bert Adkins in the 1947 production of *Papa Is All* by Patterson Greene, directed by Arthur Clare.
PHOTO: KARSH

ate some of the atmosphere of a club and if (members) assume the role of full membership we shall all profit in the process."[5]

The theatre-going public and the existing membership responded to the call. Listings in the theatre newsletter noting the number of new members signed up by campaign workers probably roused their competitive spirit. Special events, such as a lecture by "that distinguished English dramatist and man of letters Mr. J.B. Priestley,"[6] helped to heighten general interest. By 1957, subscriptions had shot up to 3,400, a reflection of "a growing demand for little theatre entertainment (in the face of competing mediums such as television)."[7]

As well as doubling its membership that year, Ottawa Little Theatre doubled its production schedule. It replaced the previous season format of four or five plays with two series of four plays each and gave subscribers the option of selecting either one or both sets of plays. "The Popular Series [was] designed for playgoers primarily interested in entertainment, while the Festival Series [catered] to tastes for distinctive types of theatre."[8] The opening play of the 1957 Popular Series was *The Teahouse of the August Moon* by John Patrick, a production that carried its own memorable incident, recalls long-time member Kevin Conlon. "One evening a bat decided to visit the teahouse during a performance," he says. "None of the young ladies on stage panicked, although some of them confessed afterwards that they were terrified. The

5. Note in program of *When We Are Married* by J. B. Priestley, October 31-November 5, 1955.
6. Ottawa Little Theatre Newletter, Vol. 2, No. 5, January 1957, p. 3. The lecture was presented at Ottawa Little Theatre on February 25, 1957.
7. Unsigned report to the Board of Directors, November 29, 1957.
8. *Ibid.*

Huguette (Beaucaire) White in the title role of the 1953 production of *Gigi*, Anita Loos' dramatization of Colette's novel, directed by Ruth Ruggles. PHOTO: VAN

audience wove back and forth as the poor, frightened creature swooped around the auditorium, finally making one last circuit around the teahouse before disappearing."

Lillian Hellman's adaptation of *The Lark* by Jean Anouilh, the final play in Festival Series that season, was more sedate as well as more intellectual.

The doubled programme of eight major plays is planned to present a balanced variety of theatre and to afford further opportunities for the young or inexperienced to gain experience in the many activities which go together to make up little theatre work.[9]

Resident stage manager Bill Adkins was lukewarm in his response to the new format. "We try to do plays to please our audiences here," he said in 1963.[10] "People want to be entertained. They like to laugh. If you start to do plays with a message, some people might love them, but not the majority."

He compared the enthusiastic response to *A Button Missing* by local playwright George Blackburn (a play in the Popular Series) with the relatively cool reaction to John Steinbeck's *Of Mice and Men*, the Festival Series offering that followed it in 1963. His dismissive tone (almost a sniff of contempt) leaves little doubt about the style of play that he preferred.

9. *Ibid.*
10. From an audio tape of an interview with Grace Lydiatt Shaw in the National Archives of Canada.

Elizabeth Hicks in the title role of the 1952 production of *Sabrina Fair* by Samuel Taylor, directed by Gwendolyn Blair and Michael Meiklejohn. Maurice the Cockatoo shares the spotlight. *PHOTO: VAN*

For a few seasons, the shows of the two series alternated rather than running in repertory. Patrons could subscribe to either or both groupings. "It just didn't work," recalls Kevin Conlon, who first joined Ottawa Little Theatre in 1954. "People didn't buy the Festival Series."[11]

Nevertheless, the theatre persevered with its two-series format into the 1960s, before returning to a single long series. A casualty along the way was the Workshop. One of its aims had been to provide opportunities for newcomers to the theatre. That aim had been incorporated in the reasoning for expanding and bifurcating the mainstage productions. And, from a practical point of view, there was simply insufficient room for the experimental group as mainstage activity increased, particularly when play runs were extended. In the 1950s, they ran for five nights each. By 1963, that had expanded to eight nights. Today, each of the eight shows of the winter season runs for 18 nights and the two summer shows play for 13 nights apiece.

11. The Festival Series may not have attracted as many single-ticket buyers, but an overview of the 50th anniversary season by Jean Southworth of the *Ottawa Journal*, April 6, 1963, notes that in the previous season "there were close to 2,500 subscribers to the Festival Series and over 3,000 to the Popular Series."

A replacement for the Workshop was a new, very little theatre at Ottawa Little Theatre. Designed by Stan White, the Theatre Under the Stairs, a "sophisticated, intimate place,"[12] was developed in the theatre basement.

> *Formerly a rehearsal room, with limited facilities, the magic of Stan White, architect-set designer, and the willing hands of Workshop members...transformed an unattractive basement into a charming and very piquant miniature theatre. Seating 71 people, it has a semi-circular stage, 22 feet wide which projects 11 feet. Four rows of chairs surround it to accommodate the audience. It is very like the ancient Greek theatre on a small scale....Experimental plays will be performed here....A new conception of theatre should emerge which could be exhilarating.*[13]

The digging in the basement, apparently caused an emergence of another kind. Excavations uncovered some tombstones and bones in the former crypt of the old church that had been transformed into the theatre. "The name 'Martha' could be seen on one of the tombstones, which led people to believe that the place was haunted by someone named Martha," says Kevin Conlon. "I remember once I was downstairs painting a canvas banner to go outside the theatre. I was the only person in the building, but I distinctly heard footsteps cross the stage and go downstairs."[14] Ten years after the event, he clearly

Roland McNicoll and Douglas Hartt in the 1957 production of *Thieves' Carnival* by Jean Anouilh, translated by Lucienne Hill, directed by William Armstrong. *PHOTO: VAN*

12. Feature by Gladys Blair, *Ottawa Journal*, August 21, 1960.
13. *Ibid.*
14. Feature by Barbara Crook, *Ottawa Citizen*, October 24, 1987.

remembers his reactions. “Did I leave very fast? You bet I did,” he says. “I dropped my paintbrush and fled, breaking all records getting out of there.”

There have been other sightings of Martha, the theatre ghost, over the years. “I’ve heard footsteps many, many times and put my tools away and tried not to run,” says resident stage manager Ken McGill. “In the old days, you’d walk across the stage and in the silence of the theatre you could imagine a presence,” says actor Bill Luxton. “It could be eerie.” Eerie enough that many theatre members avoid being alone in the building late at night, in case they are confronted by the spirit of the woman said to have been an unwed mother refused shelter (and later burial in consecrated ground) by the church.

Another ‘Martha’ tale tells of her connection with an actress who died on stage in the 1960s. “The story goes that the clock in Bill Adkin’s office stopped working at the exact moment that she died,” says board member Val Bogan. (Did Martha stop the clock?) “When the play was redone twenty years later, the clock started working again—at the same time that she had died.”

A bat joined the cast of the 1957 production of *The Teahouse of the August Moon* by John Patrick, directed by George Palmer. *PHOTO: VAN*

Florence Fancott in the 1958 production of *The Lark* by Jean Anouilh, adapted by Lillian Hellman, directed by George Palmer. *PHOTO: VAN*

Martha may be apocryphal. Sceptic Douglas Cooke, husband of Sybil and an Ottawa Little Theatre member since 1954, is sure that she is. "Bill Adkins was the main supporter of Martha," he says. "He practically lived at the theatre and must have heard the old building creak and groan," he says. Indeed that may explain some of the sounds, but not the accounts of cast members over the years who are certain that they have heard organ music when they are alone in the theatre, or glimpsed a flowing, white figure in the wings or been sure that they are being watched when the theatre is empty. Or perhaps it is simply traditional for every theatre to have a ghost. Real or imagined, Martha remains part of the Ottawa Little Theatre tradition.

So does the style of play that audiences favour. From the beginning, the emphasis was on respectability. "There was a time when we couldn't say on stage that a woman was pregnant—any mention of her having a baby had to be cut out," recalled Betty Cruikshank in 1969. "Things have changed thankfully...(but)

I doubt if we'll ever see nudity on the stage of our theatre."[15] In the 1990s, there's the occasional flash—two almost bare rears in the 1996 production of Ray Cooney's *Out of Order*, for instance—but the emphasis remains on traditional fare, traditionally presented. The aim is to "give the audience what it wants,"[16] says Jane Murray, Ottawa Little Theatre's president for more than a quarter of a century (from 1964 to 1989). "If the seats aren't filled, there's no income." Such a consideration is of central importance for a theatre that has always functioned without grants and remains proud of its financial independence.

Effective fundraising campaigns in the past had bought Ottawa Little Theatre its own building in 1928. "In those days," recalled Bill Adkins, "Everybody did everything. I did props, helped move the furniture—everything."[17] "Now we've grown up. Anything that has to be done we can afford to pay for."[18] By the 1960s, the theatre had a paid staff of five or six to care for the building and the office and to build and manage the productions. Operating expenses were covered by revenue from plays. But close to forty years after Ottawa Little Theatre had moved into its own building, the theatre needed a major facelift, particularly as the National Arts Centre, the major facility intended to be the nation's artistic showplace, was to open its doors in 1969.

> *Little Theatre officials...approached several sources in the hope of getting grants to help renovate the theatre, but without success. The Canada Council [could] not give money for capital expenditure, nor [did] it have allowances for operating expenses in what is strictly an amateur house. The same is true of the Ontario Arts Council which, though sympathetic, [had] no system under which it [could] grant money to an enterprise such as this.*
>
> *"If we had all the sympathy in dollars and cents," a theatre spokesman said wryly, "we could carry out all our projects."*[19]

And even though the theatre owned its building outright and had paid off all its bond-holders, it proved "impossible to raise a mortgage on the building because of

15. "Pioneer Reminisces" by Sheila McCook, *Ottawa Citizen*, August 6, 1969, *op. cit.*
16. Feature by Audrey Ashley, *Ottawa Citizen*, February 1, 1982.
17. Interview with Audrey Ashley, *Ottawa Citizen*, Janurary 27, 1968, *op. cit.*
18. Audio tape of 1965 interview with Grace Lydiatt Shaw, *National Archives of Canada*, op. cit.
19. "Ottawa Little Theatre Knows How to Succeed" by Audrey Ashley, *Ottawa Citizen*, May 18, 1968.

its sentimental value—'nobody would foreclose if it became necessary.'"[20]

It was time for the second major fundraising campaign in Ottawa Little Theatre's history. By 1969, expansions to the lobby and foyer, new carpeting and upgraded seating, which cost some $70,000, were paid in full. Neither audiences nor performers had much time to enjoy the improvements to their building, however, before the great fire of 1970 totally destroyed the theatre.

20. *Ibid.*

CHAPTER 5

Fire and Rebirth

This place runs on love, but it's fire that has made our progress.
Jane Murray, President
Ottawa Little Theatre
(1964-1989)

Two great fires lighted the way for Ottawa Little Theatre over the years and translated into two significant stages in its development. The first forced the group out of rented space at the Victoria Museum[1] and set its members on a quest to build a theatre of their own. The second was the reason for building a new theatre—a facility that, more than a quarter of a century later, is still admired and envied by amateur and professional theatres across the country.

"If the Parliament Buildings hadn't been burned down, maybe [the original Ottawa Drama League] would just have sat around in the Museum and never done anything. But once you have a debt you can't just throw up your hands. You own something, and you have to make it work," said Jane Murray in 1978.[2]

However, it would have been hard to convince any of Ottawa Little Theatre's members—then numbering more than five thousand—that the disastrous fire of July 1, 1970 could have a positive side.

"It was a tragedy, an absolute tragedy," recalls Kevin Conlon. "We practically wept. We thought it was the end."

"I hadn't seen a newspaper or listened to the radio," says Marian Bray, a long-time theatre member who was at her summer cottage on the day of the fire. "I was

1. Parliament commandeered the space at the museum in 1916 while the House of Commons was being rebuilt. See Chapter 1.
2. "50 Years of Love—Little Theatre Grows Through Fire" by Audrey Ashley, *Ottawa Citizen*, January 3, 1978.

back at my office the next day and had some of the next season's brochures on my desk. I remember offering one to the first person who came in. She said, 'Haven't you heard? The theatre burned down yesterday.' I still remember the chill I felt. It was a terrible shock."

"A group of us had gone to Stratford for the opening night of Paddy (Patrick) Crean's one-man show, *The Sun Never Sets*," recalls Lorraine St. Laurent, another long-time theatre member who was out of town on the fateful day. "Then we had a phone call to tell us 'the theatre burned down last night.' I remember just how upset we all were. We drove straight back to Ottawa and down to the theatre to see the awful sight."

By the time they arrived, the theatre was no more than a pile of smouldering rubble. The fire, which had begun in the Green Room, had demolished the building in less than three hours, "destroying props, costumes, sets and valuable records. The cause of the fire was never determined, although investigators suspected it might

The fire that began in the Green Room on July 1, 1970 completely destroyed the theatre. Almost immediately after the disaster the rebuilding campaign began. PHOTO: Courtesy of *Ottawa Citizen*

have been the result of electrical malfunctions or firecrackers tossed through the basement window by children taking part in the Dominion Day celebrations."[3]

Because July 1 was a public holiday, the theatre was empty, part of the reason that the alarm had not been raised immediately, so giving the fire time to take hold. Even stage manager Bill Adkins, the man everyone called 'Mr. OLT,' was away that day. "He was in Victoria," recalls broadcaster Charles Haines, a member of the board of directors at the time of the fire. "We were very concerned about calling to tell him. But he took it remarkably well, considering how much the theatre meant to him." Like so many others for whom Ottawa Little Theatre was a home away from home, he returned immediately to view the burned-out remnants of the building and more than fifty years of memories. As the news stories describing the disaster pointed out, this fire meant much "more than the loss of a landmark building."[4]

3. "The Little Theatre that Thrives" by Barbara Crook, *Ottawa Citizen*, October 24, 1987.
4. "1500 Watch Blaze," *Ottawa Citizen*, July 2, 1970.

The fire was able to gain a decisive hold on the 97-year-old stone and frame building before passersby detected smoke escaping from under the eaves and from windows.

Mrs. Gladys Tremblay of 228 Besserer Street said she and her family were finishing coffee at 10:40 p.m. when an unidentified young girl pounded on the door and said the theatre was on fire.

[Fire] Chief [Phil] Larkin said his crews from number three station on nearby Cumberland Street arrived to find the building engulfed in flames. He said firemen were unable to enter the theatre because of dense smoke.

The building burned spectacularly during the first hour, flames often leaping 50 feet above the sharply peaked roof. Smoke was visible throughout most of the city.[5]

As more than fifteen hundred people watched, the building went "up in smoke and down in ashes....By 11:30 p.m. only charred beams remained of the roof and the blaze was mostly contained within the stone walls. Trouble spots continued to flare up in various parts of the building....The fire continued burning in the full

Architect's rendering of design for the new theatre by Ted Fancott.

5. "$100,000 Fire 'Curtains' for Little Theatre" by Angus Ricker, *Ottawa Citizen*, July 2, 1970.

basement of the building where the props, costumes and furniture were stored until well after 1 a.m."[6]

"The whole thing was a mass of rubble," recalls Charles Haines. "Sitting on a tilt on one pile was the theatre safe. All it had in it was 12 bottles of champagne. That showed what we thought the safe was good for and the kind of (trusting, fun-loving) people that theatre people were. The champagne was for the next opening night. As I recall, we sat down and drank some while we decided what to do next."

"Many people thought...that...amateur theatre had had its day," said Jane Murray, "that maybe we should take the money from the insurance and help people in the theatre with scholarships."[7]

"There was talk that the National Arts Centre would smother us," recalls Mr. Haines. "It was part of the first superficial wave of discussion that the fire was the end of OLT. That didn't last though. We sat around cheering each other up and finally decided that theatre generates more theatre (which is what has happened)."

President Jane Murray and architect W.E. (Ted) Fancott on the site of the new theatre-in-progress.

6. "1,500 Watch Blaze," *op. cit.*
7. "50 Years of Love—Little Theatre Grows Through Fire," *op. cit.*

The National Arts Centre, intended as the country's performing-arts showplace, had opened the previous year. Professional theatre was thriving in other centres, often the transmuted offspring of long-standing amateur theatre groups. For example, community theatres in Winnipeg and Calgary had been transformed with the birth of the Manitoba Theatre Centre in the 1950s and Theatre Calgary (formerly MAC 14 Workshop Theatre) in the 1960s.

The Dominion Drama Festival (renamed Theatre Canada in 1970) still existed, but was no longer of major importance to Ottawa Little Theatre. The travelling festival, which was to continue until 1978, was waning as professional theatre in Canada grew. Even as far back as 1948, the first time that the festival returned to Ottawa Little Theatre after its initial, very influential decade, it had not recaptured the early glory of the years before World War II.

Seeing how the theatrical climate had changed across the nation, it was not surprising that some Ottawa Little Theatre members had doubts about the future. "I never did," said Jane Murray.[8] Heartbroken as she had been—"and she *was* heartbroken when she saw the damage," says Charles Haines—she was determined to rebuild.

"Jane Murray and (board member) Len Holt were instrumental in getting the theatre going again," said Kevin Conlon, who, under Len Holt's direction, was to play the lead in Peter Luke's *Hadrian VII*, the first production in the rebuilt theatre. "The other directors (board members) had their doubts about whether we could start again after the fire, but Len and Jane were a tremendous team."[9]

"It didn't take long for us to decide that Ottawa Little Theatre still had a place in the community," says Charles Haines. "Len was the one who was the most optimistic from the beginning. He kept all our spirits up. And Jane was tireless in her efforts."

"Smoke was still rising from the charred embers of the Ottawa Little Theatre when the decision was made: 'Rebuild!' The community rallied to the support of its local theatre."[10] Now began the most intensive fundraising campaign in the theatre's history. "I think I may have presented the first cheque when we decided to rebuild," recalls Marian Bray. Although a little more than $300,000 had been recouped from the fire insurance covering the building, and the group owned the land on which it had stood, another $445,000 was needed for the new structure.

8. *Ottawa Citizen*, January 3, 1978, *op. cit.*
9. "The Little Theatre that Thrives" by Barbara Crook, *Ottawa Citizen*, October 24, 1987, *op. cit.*
10. "Sixty Years of Memories," *Performing Arts in Canada Magazine*, Summer 1973, p. 25.

Even before the fundraising campaign was officially launched, supporters organized a television tribute to their theatre. Conceived by CBC producer Bill Armstrong, who had acted and directed at Ottawa Little Theatre, the program, which aired on September 10, 1970, was billed as a "cooperative community project."

> *Offers of assistance came from producers, writers, actors and musicians—all free of charge—when they heard about Mr. Armstrong's idea for a special show recalling the historic role OLT has played in the community and its contribution to Canadian theatre....Performing unions waived all rules to allow members to participate.*[11]

Produced by Bill Glenn, a former director of Ottawa Little Theatre's Theatre for Children, the tribute was filmed at the National Arts Centre. It featured selections from the highly successful *Little Theatre Revue* of 1942, with many of the original cast members repeating their roles, and interviews with Amelia Hall, Yousuf Karsh, Rich Little (filmed on location in Las Vegas) and "others who feel they owe much of their success to early association with the theatre."[12] A similar show was aired as a CJOH Telethon.

Among those who appeared in the tribute was Florence Fancott, one of the group's most successful actresses. "I spoke the first words on the new stage," she recalls. "It wasn't a very big or important part, but still they were the first words."

She and her architect husband, Ted, had been members of Ottawa Little Theatre since moving to Ottawa in 1949. Mr. Fancott, who designed the sets for numerous productions over the years, was to design the new theatre in his professional capacity as the senior partner of W.E. Fancott and Bett Architects. "And he didn't have a hefty architect's fee because he was a member," notes Charles Haines, who had provided the voice-over for the television tribute.

Less than six months after the fire, Jane Murray announced that the rebuilding project would begin on February 8, 1971 and that the new Ottawa Little Theatre would open its next season in the new theatre that fall. "Rebuilding fund chairman Kenneth C. Binks announced that 24 per cent of the fund's goal (of $445,000) had been pledged in the first month of the campaign. 'This is the first time in 57 years

11. "Artists Pay Tribute to OLT," *Ottawa Citizen*, September 5, 1970.
12. *Ibid.*

we have had to ask for public help,' he said....'The Little Theatre has given so much to help the community. We feel we'll have no difficulty reaching our goal.'"[13]

He was partially right. Ottawa Little Theatre did achieve its goal, but not without an assortment of financial and bureaucratic problems along the way. First, the regional government refused to issue a building permit, deciding instead to expropriate a 10-foot strip of land for 100 feet along the west side of King Edward Avenue, to protect "the right of way for future widening"[14] of the street. That order proved costly, even though the theatre was paid $20,000 for the expropriated land. The cost of redesigning and re-engineering the new building far exceeded that amount.

"'We've lost eight per cent of the land,' said Mr. Fancott, 'It has made the planning of a theatre on that site very difficult.'...(He) said squeezing the theatre onto the truncated site would require more excavation and result in added expenses."[15]

By the next week, the headline in the *Ottawa Citizen* was "Theatre Overcomes Problem," demonstrating the group's customary reaction to difficulties. However, costs had increased substantially. Response to the call for funds, which included the sale of life memberships at $1,000 each, was good, but still fell $200,000 short of the $750,000 needed to complete the building.

A mortgage seemed the obvious answer, but obtaining a mortgage was not easy—Ottawa Little Theatre had been turned down before, when seeking funds to renovate the old building shortly before the fire. President Jane Murray, an iron lady with a mission, would not give up. "My mother was largely responsible for raising the money for the theatre," says her daughter Janet Banigan, recalling how Mrs. Murray persuaded the Bank of Nova Scotia to provide a $200,000 mortgage and then strove to raise the money to pay it off—a feat accomplished within five years. (The theatre has been mortgage-free ever since.)

Meanwhile, performances continued in colleges and high schools around the city.[16] Construction went ahead.[17] "Len Holt was the driving force there," says Kevin Conlon. "It's because of Len that Ottawa Little Theatre was one of the first—if not the first—public buildings in the city to have a handicapped washroom, for instance."

13. "Rebuilding Starts Next Month," *Ottawa Citizen*, January 20, 1971.
14. "Littler or Costlier Theatre is Question," *Ottawa Citizen*, April 23, 1971.
15. *Ibid.*
16. Primarily at Algonquin College and LaSalle Academy.
17. The construction of the theatre was the first major job for M. P. Lundy Construction. President Mike Lundy still holds season tickets. His first set for the inaugural season in the new theatre were a gift from Len Holt.

"He—together with Jane Murray—was responsible for there being a new theatre," adds his wife, Elizabeth. "Actor, director and all-round theatre person, he just loved the theatre."

With Len Holt as the symbol of optimism, Jane Murray that of determination, and a solid core of support from the membership and the city, the seemingly impossible happened. Just 19 months after the fire that had razed the building, the new theatre was ready for the public. The audience took their seats for the first performance of Peter Luke's *Hadrian VII*, directed by Len Holt, on February 10, 1972, unaware that behind the scenes, actors, who had rehearsed in freezing conditions during construction, had to step over piles of rubble in the dressing room and clamber over unfinished steps on to the stage. The audience was equally unaware that "the workmen had been there all of the last two days (one a Sunday) working free of charge to make sure that the public areas were ready."[18] The carpet in the foyer had been laid that very afternoon, just a few hours before curtain time.

"'Every brick is a furrow up here,' said director Leonard Holt, tapping his forehead. 'It's been blood, sweat and tears all the way.'"[19] The audience knew none of that. Neither were they meant to know. In the tradition of the magic of theatre, they saw only the stately procession gliding down the aisle of the splendid new auditorium.

"'I picked that play because...it opened with the cardinals walking down the centre aisle with the house lights on,' recalls (Mrs.) Murray. 'I thought it would be nice if the audience didn't have to sit in the dark for those first few moments.'"[20]

It provided a little extra time to see the splendour of the new theatre. "Even those who deeply lament the demise of the old theatre can't help but admire the new stage facilities," wrote *Ottawa Citizen* reporter Audrey Ashley after touring the building just before its official opening.[21]

> *The stage itself is 80 feet in width, which means there is wing space undreamed of in the old building. (The stage opening itself is 34 feet in width.) The grid is 45 feet above the stage, and stage manager Bill Adkins points out joyously that this means three or four sets could be "flown" if necessary.*
>
> *Lighting is set up from a booth at stage left, and there is a control console in the lighting and sound board which runs across the back of the auditorium*

18. Comment from Charles Haines, who also said that the work crew were prepared to waive union rules because of their loyalty to Len Holt.
19. "Curtain Goes Up on Ottawa Little Theatre" by Audrey Ashley, *Ottawa Citizen*, January 29, 1972.
20. "The Little Theatre that Thrives," *Ottawa Citizen, op. cit.*
21. "Curtain Goes Up on Ottawa Little Theatre," *Ottawa Citizen, op. cit.*

and is reached by means of a spiral staircase leading to a catwalk all along the side of the theatre.

There are three traps in the stage floor: two large ones to take care of scenery and furniture and a smaller one for actors to use when special effects are required.

Beneath the stage are all the working facilities—a prop room, a "green room" for the actors, with a small kitchen attached, and a rehearsal room which must be a director's delight—a space 43 feet by 30 feet, which will accommodate an entire stage set.

Dressing rooms are positively elegant, complete with vanities and tiled showers, and a large costume room has space to accommodate, eventually, double-decker racks of clothes as well as shelves for shoes, hat boxes and other accessories.

...There's much to admire in this new, up-dated version of the Little Theatre.

The outside walls are finished with warm, reddish-brown brick...and the ground-floor lobby, with its red tiled floor, contains generous...space....To the left of the lobby is a staircase which follows the curve of a brick wall to the upper foyer—a large pleasant space with long windows all along one side....The whole lobby [is] carpeted in red... Steps lead to two smaller foyers on either side...It's from [here] that one enters the auditorium, and the similarity in atmosphere between this auditorium and the old one is startling....Here again, the dominant color—indeed, the only color—is red: warm red carpet, red walls, and red upholstery on the 510 seats. The floor is steeply raked...and the seats are staggered, giving extremely good sightlines from practically any part of the house.[22]

"We took advantage of the fire to make the most of the space we had," says Sybil Cooke, who has been Ottawa Little Theatre president since 1990. "Our intention has always been to make the theatre a welcoming place to visit." Now with close to nine thousand season-ticket holders and numerous single-ticket buyers, there are many to acknowledge that the 'welcome' is firmly in place.

22. *Ibid.*

CHAPTER 6

Putting Out Smaller Fires

A little fire is quickly trodden out.
William Shakespeare
in *King Henry VI, Part III*

With the completion of the new building, Ottawa Little Theatre had successfully weathered the greatest storm in its lengthy history. "Five years after it opened, [the building] was also paid for—no grants, no government subsidies, no government handouts of any kind."[1]

The theatre's financial success was closely related to "one simple programming policy: Give audiences what they want to see. 'The audience is paying the bills and we have to listen to what they like... The main thing is to please those 510 people in those 510 seats every night,' [said] Jane Murray"[2] in 1987.

With that in mind, occasional calls for more *avant-garde* fare tended to go unheeded. Shows that had been successful elsewhere or had been part of an earlier Ottawa Little Theatre season appeared most frequently. "The repertoire is a tried-and-true mixture of comedies, farces, thrillers and classical dramas. Coarse language is rare, as are controversial subjects," wrote Barbara Crook in 1987.[3] Ten years later, the style is similar. The 1997-98 season begins with a musical: *A Funny Thing Happened on the Way to the Forum* by Burt Shevelove and Larry Gelbart with music by Stephen Sondheim, and continues with an assortment of well-known dramas, comedies and farces: *Tea and Sympathy* by Robert Anderson; *My Three Angels* by Bella and Samuel Spewack; *The Heiress* by Ruth and Augustus Goetz;

1. "Burned Out a Decade Ago, OLT Thrives" by Audrey Ashley, *Ottawa Citizen*, February 1, 1982.
2. "The Little Theatre that Thrives," *Ottawa Citizen*, *op. cit.*
3. *Ibid.*

The Saturday Players' 1953 production of Jean Giraudoux's *The Mad Woman of Chaillot*, directed by Julia Murphy, won the Eastern Ontario regional Drama Festival Award for best production.
PHOTO: VAN

My Giddy Aunt by Ray Cooney and John Chapman; *The Middle Ages* by A.R. Gurney; *The Trip to Bountiful* by Horton Foote; and *Don't Dress for Dinner* by Marc Camoletti.

"I always tried to give our audiences the chance to see plays that have been performed on Broadway or in the West End (of London), at reasonable prices," said Jane Murray in 1995.

Some performers look down on (Ottawa Little Theatre) productions while resenting the full houses that attend the OLT shows and not their own. They complain about the conservatism of the play selection, and dismiss it as being content to run mediocre copies of established hits. From Jane Murray's point of view, her mandate is what is important: "What we try to do is please our audience. If we can't please all eight thousand at once, maybe we can please them five out of seven times."

Since Murray's role in the play selection is so important (she chooses and presents a list of plays for approval to a committee)...she travels a great deal

Bruce Swerdfager and Joyce Taylor in the 1953 production of William Shakespeare's *Merry Wives of Windsor,* directed by Michael Meiklejohn.

PHOTO: VAN

to see theatre in other countries, and doesn't mind controversy. But, above all, she feels the OLT has a commitment to pleasing its audience. If that sounds overly cautious, Murray leaves you with one more thought: "If you come down here for a few years, you'll be able to talk about the plays that are being written and talked about in the theatre centres like New York and London." For 69 years, it has been obvious that Ottawa has room for a theatre with that mandate.[4]

"There's nothing as shaky as this theatre business and you just have to please the audience—it's as commercial as that," Jane Murray said again and again. "If the audiences are not pleased and entertained, they're not going to come. And without grants of any kind, thc theatre would be in deep trouble because it's a very expensive place to run."[5]

"And I have kept on the course that Jane set," says current president Sybil

4. "The OLT Continues to Please Its Audience" by Richard Ager, *Ottawa Revue*, August 20-26, 1981.
5. "50 Years of Love—Little Theatre Grows Through Fire," *Ottawa Citizen, op. cit.*

Nancy Howard in the 1960 production of *Bus Stop* by William Inge, directed by Anthony Tyler.

Valerie Beveridge and Leonard Holt in the 1966 production of *The Private Ear and the Public Eye* by Peter Shaffer, directed by Kevin Conlon.
PHOTO: Courtesy Kevin and Elizabeth Conlon

Rich Little (left) and Tom Dunlevie in *Bus Stop*.

Cooke. "There is a strong argument for more Canadian plays and we try to include one every season, but it doesn't always work out."

> *Yet there is (still) a feeling among some of OLT's more active members that the programming ought to be more venturesome. 'Actors like something they can get their teeth into,' observes one.*
>
> *Another says that the average OLT audience doesn't like to be made to think or to look into themselves or society, but suggests that over a period of time it might be possible to attract a new and possibly younger audience by introducing more adventurous plays.*[6]

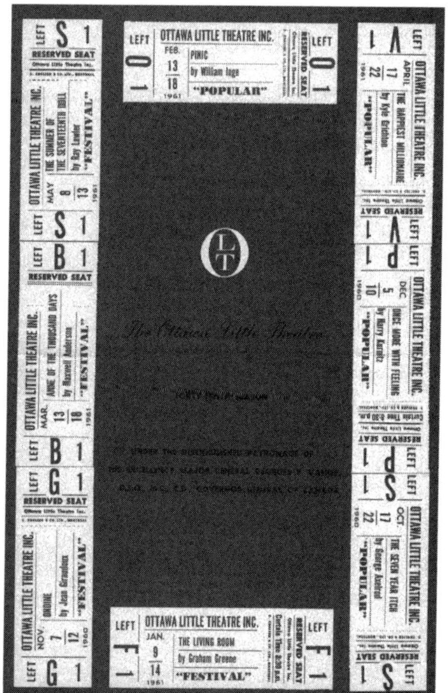

The two-series format of the 1960s was a partial answer to such an argument. When the Popular Series proved considerably more popular than the more cerebral programming of the Festival Series, a return to a single, lighter tone became inevitable. By the time Ottawa Little Theatre was established in its new building, the preferred programming style seemed firmly set, though reporter Audrey Ashley noted in 1981 that "the Ottawa Little Theatre may have taken to heart the frequent criticism aimed at its choice of plays. Or perhaps they've been encouraged by the success of two of this season's meatier offerings—Arnold Wesker's *Roots*, and Maxwell Anderson's epic *Elizabeth the Queen*. In any event, plans for the 1981-82 season look encouraging."[7] On balance, though, lighter shows were the most likely to play to sold-out houses. That reality and the rising subscription numbers, to more than nine thousand by 1987, made it difficult for the board of directors to justify any radical change in programming. Today, houses are still full and the theatre has

6. "Burned Out a Decade Ago, OLT Thrivies," *Ottawa Citizen, op. cit.*
7. "Ottawa Little Theatre Plans Meatier Season" by Audrey Ashley, *Ottawa Citizen*, April 3, 1981. The 1981-82 season included Terence Rattigan's *Cause Celebre*, Tennessee William's *Summer and Smoke* and an original by Ottawa playwright/civil servant Chris Burke, *Don't Despair, Fonctionnaire.*

between eight thousand and nine thousand subscribers each year. The slight drop in the last ten years can be attributed to the "greying" of the audience, although many of the older members continue a family tradition by willing or donating their season tickets to the next generation.

Had Ottawa Little Theatre turned professional in the 1960s, as many other community theatres across the country did, such a tradition might not be part of its community spirit today. In fact, one of long-time stage manager Bill Adkins' pet peeves was the suggestion that Ottawa Little Theatre should become a professional company. "He [believed] the theatre in its present form fills an important need in the community, providing an outlet for people who love the theatre but cannot work in it full-time, and acting as a very necessary training ground for youngsters with an interest in the stage."[8]

The Centennial Play—actually three plays by Robertson Davies, W.O. Mitchell and Eric Nicol respectively—was produced by Ottawa Little Theatre in association with the Canadian Festival of the Arts on January 11, 1967 to celebrate Canada's 100th birthday.

"If we had become professional, we couldn't afford to keep the ticket prices so reasonable," said Jane Murray in 1995. "We wouldn't be serving the community. We wouldn't be Ottawa Little Theatre."

She also resisted occasional calls for professional directors for the same reasons. Adds Sybil Cooke, "We hear that less often now, probably because as we have progressed over the years, our own directors have improved."

They have, after all, had the opportunity to develop their skills in a top-quality facility, a place that feels like home for performers and audience. And it feels that way, because Ottawa Little Theatre has always been aware of its public and its mandate. The return is the long-standing loyalty of that public, a loyalty tested and proven during the fundraising campaigns to renovate the old theatre and build anew after the 1970 fire. It was tested again when the theatre was faced with an unexpected and hefty tax bill of $21,531 in 1983.[9]

8. "Bill Adkins Remembers Them All," *Ottawa Citizen, op. cit.*
9. Because the old theatre had been a converted church and religious buildings are tax-exempt, Ottawa Little Theatre had not been required to pay school taxes on the property in the past.

The theatre escaped taxes on its King Edward Avenue property for most of its history, but in 1980, the city of Ottawa decided that the theatre was not eligible for continued exemption because it does not administer to the poor.[10]

The theatre appealed, pointing out that it had never received any financial support from any level of government. That had been officially acknowledged just one year earlier, when it had received a $2,500 award from Ottawa-Carleton Regional Council in recognition of its artistic contribution and self-sustaining status. But "appeals to the City of Ottawa and the provincial government for forgiveness of the tax [were] unsuccessful."[11]

Some city councillors...say exempting the OLT would establish an undesirable precedent, and maintain that the theatre should seek a grant if it wants relief from taxation.

The first of these objections is simply silly; under a 1929 City of Ottawa Act, the OLT is already exempt from regular municipal taxation, though it does pay local improvement and sewer levies. The precedent, in other words, is already there.

The second concern reflects the view of some councillors that grants are a better way of supporting worthy organizations than are tax breaks. This may be so as a general principle. But the OLT situation is unique; any principle that cannot be bent to deal with the exceptional is not a principle, but inflexible dogma.

The volunteers who run the Little Theatre take great pride in the fact that they have never sought or received direct government support—not even when the old theatre building burned down in the early 1970s. City council should acknowledge its contribution to the community with its support.[12]

Ottawa Little Theatre solved its immediate financial problem by asking its members for help. A donation of $10 from each subscriber "would cover the theatre's needs, and would enable it to continue to operate without grants...as it always has," pointed out Jane Murray.[13] The members came through and the tax bill was paid.

10. "OBE Throwing Support Behind Little Theatre" by Bert Hill, *Ottawa Citizen*, August 28, 1984.
11. "Little Theatre Asks Members for Extra $10," *Ottawa Citizen*, March 4, 1983.
12. "Theatre doesn't need a tax encore," *Ottawa Citizen* editorial, November 21, 1984.
13. "Little Theatre Asks Members for Extra $10," *Ottawa Citizen, op. cit.*

The following year, the theatre was granted its tax exemption when a private member's bill, presented by Ottawa MPP Evelyn Gigantes, passed in the provincial legislature.[14]

Now tax-exempt but still without any direct financial support from any level of government, Ottawa Little Theatre has the backing of a long list of individual donors and life members and occasional corporate sponsors. But ticket sales remain its primary source of income. True to its tradition, it keeps prices low so that it can preserve its mission to entertain and retain its special place in the community—a status acknowledged by Donald MacSween, then Director General of the National Arts Centre, in a congratulatory telegram in 1983:

> *At the beginning of your eighth decade from a very much junior performing arts organization to the finest little theatre in North America in homage and with the hope that in time we shall achieve in the professional field the long and honoured contribution you have in the amateur field.*

14. Private member's bills are rarely successful. The success of this bill, which was supported by the Ottawa Board of Education and Ottawa City Council, was, in itself, a measure of the esteem in which Ottawa Little Theatre was held.

Holly Larocque, Peter Cochrane and Denis Laviolette in the 1978 production of the Anthony Newley/Leslie Bricusse musical *The Roar of the Greasepaint, The Smell of the Crowd,* directed by Joseph Shaver, with musical direction by Derek Stannard and choreography by Mitzi Hauser.

Sharon McGee and Peter Smith in the 1970 production of *The Paisley Convertible* by Harry Cauley.
PHOTO: Courtesy Kevin and Elizabeth Conlon

The 1982 Ottawa Little Theatre production of Chris Burke's adaptation of *A Christmas Carol* by Charles Dickens was televised by the Canadian Broadcasting Corporation for presentation across the country. Ottawa Little Theatre remounted the show in 1993. Senator Royce Frith played the role of Ebeneezer Scrooge.

Barry Caiger and Don Quiring in the 1996 production of *A Coat of Varnish* by Ronald Millar.
PHOTO: Michael Vuckovic

Charles Kerr and Kevin Conlon in the 1974 production of *The Patrick Pearse Motel* by Hugh Leonard.
PHOTO: Courtesy Kevin and Elizabeth Conlon

Françoise Tardy and Kevin Conlon in the 1984 production of *Pajama Tops* by Jean De Letraz, Mawby Green and Ed Feilbert.
PHOTO: Courtesy Kevin and Elizabeth Conlon

Mary Gore and David Howard in the 1996 production of *Crown Matrimonial* by Royce Ryton, directed by Joan Sullivan Eady.
PHOTO: Michael Vuckovic

CHAPTER 7

By the People, for the People

The way that they played together
was beautiful to see.
Henry Cuyler Bunner
in *One, Two, Three*

Our grateful thanks...to the loyal folk...
Who gave their time and talent without stint..
Gave us...a temple for the
loveliest of the Muses.
Duncan Campbell Scott[1]

The many photographs lining the walls of Ottawa Little Theatre highlight special moments in its history. There is the church that became the theatre. Here are stage manager Bill Adkins and Elizabeth Cruikshank, who chaired the committee that raised the funds to buy the church. A little further along is a photograph of Kenneth Binks, who chaired the fundraising committee after the 1970 fire. Then there are photographs of the aftermath of the fire and the new building in progress with architect Ted Fancott, Bill Adkins and president Jane Murray on the construction site, all wearing hard hats. In the upper foyer and the Green Room are shots of awards ceremonies, productions and hundreds of pictures of actors, directors, designers and technicians across the years. Every one has left a mark. A few have shaped the theatre's history.

1. From *Prologue*, written for the opening of Ottawa Little Theatre in 1928.

PHOTO: KARSH

Father of the Family

Duncan Campbell Scott (1862-1947)

Poet, short-story writer, playwright, senior civil servant, Duncan Campbell Scott first became president of the Ottawa Drama League in 1923. Under his guidance, the group was to become "the largest organization of its kind in Canada and...among the best in the U.S. or Great Britain."[2]

Dr. Scott, the poet who ran the Department of Indian Affairs, was the major force in carrying the Ottawa Drama League into its own building in 1928. A year later, his artistic and administrative abilities converged when he approached the Ottawa Board of Control to request that the theatre be listed under "public institutions, literary and scientific" and, as a former church, be exempted from municipal taxes.

A man who was "always straight and to the point about everything,"[3] he was determined that the group should have a permanent home in a building unburdened by property taxes.[4] And, as his rise from clerk to Deputy Minister attested, when Dr. Scott made up his mind to do something, he did it.

Descriptions of Duncan Campbell Scott, bureaucrat, depict a cool, authoritarian figure. He was "typical of civil servants then and now. He was loyal to his various ministers, he never spent the public's money unwisely, and, most important, he was an efficient administrator."[5]

The people at Ottawa Little Theatre were aware of his efficiency and strength as

2. "A Fact a Day About Ottawa," *Ottawa Journal*, January 3, 1928.
3. As described by Bill Adkins in the *Ottawa Journal*, June 12, 1963.
4. Ottawa Little Theatre remains free of municipal taxes and, following a private member's bill in 1983, is also exempt from school tax payments. See Chapter 6.
5. "The Poet who ran Indian Affairs," book review by Allan Levine, *Ottawa Citizen*, February 7, 1987.

their president—a position to which he was regularly re-elected until shortly before the outbreak of World War II. But they also valued his creativity and his friendship. His play *Pierre*, later included in a collection published by Hart House, was presented at Ottawa Little Theatre. His specially prepared *Prologue* was the first piece presented on its stage at the official opening (see Appendix III).

As Elizabeth Cruikshank said at the theatre housewarming party in 1928, "This...is our first family gathering in our new home and, Dr. Scott, we want to congratulate you most loyally and lovingly....We are here as a family and you...are the father of this family. Your kindly guidance and friendly direction kept us together."[6] That night, the drama league presented their president with "a solid silver tray...as a tangible token of the general affection and appreciation in which he [was] held by everyone associated with the League."[7]

They had no doubt of the significance of his role in ensuring that they should have a home of their own.

The "Love and Whisky" Man

Colonel Henry Osborne (1874-1949)

In his professional life, Colonel Henry Campbell Osborne, lawyer and military officer, was the Secretary-General of the Canadian Agency of the Imperial War Graves Commission. For the members of Ottawa Little Theatre, the gentleman, who lived just down the road from the theatre and spent most of his free time there, was honoured for his "valuable contribution to the Drama League since its very early days [as] one of the prime organizers of the Dominion Drama Festival...known from coast to coast for his contribution to the Canadian Theatre."[8]

Colonel Osborne was vice-president of the

6. "Drama League has Pleasant House-warming in New Home," *Ottawa Journal*, January 9, 1928.
7. *Ibid.*
8. Part of vote of thanks given to Colonel Osborne when he retired from the position of vice-president of the Ottawa Drama League on June 11, 1947.

Ottawa Drama League during most of Duncan Campbell Scott's tenure. As one of the group's senior policy-makers, he, like Dr. Scott, was determined to move productions from "parish halls, obscure rooms, the Museum theatre [and into] a theatre as good as Hart House in Toronto."[9] Soon after the group had achieved this objective, Lord Bessborough, the new Governor General of Canada, determined to establish "an annual Dominion of Canada Drama Festival." Vincent Massey, the former Toronto don and amateur actor who was to become the festival's president, "suggested that the Governor General should approach Col. Henry Osborne, a mild-mannered friend of Massey's who had attended college in Port Hope, to act as director of the proposed festival....Bessborough already knew [him] as a founder of the Ottawa Drama League [and] was only too delighted to recruit such a gentlemanly volunteer....Osborne was willingly roped into the job."[10]

From then on, he worried and worked on the details to make the Dominion Drama Festival a reality. During the final preparations for the inaugural festival at Ottawa Little Theatre, "Col. H.C. Osborne, acting president of the Ottawa Drama League and vice-chairman and honorary director of the festival [was] in and out during the day, full of charming speeches and helpful suggestions."[11] He was anxious that the festival, founded, as he quipped, on "love and whisky" and taking place in the theatre he had helped to build, should be a success.

It was. And as the liaison between the Dominion Drama Festival and the Ottawa Drama League and an officer of both organizations, he had much to do with its influence on the development of drama in Canada. Some years later, when attempts were underway to revive the festival after its suspension during the war years, Colonel Osborne was in place once more. "It was a nostalgic meeting. Col. Osborne was older and less energetic but he was as courtly as ever and his very presence recalled the great days of Bessborough and Massey and the carefree fun and games of the Festival."[12] He was there for the revival in 1947. By this time retired, he was on hand again in 1948 when the Dominion Drama Festival returned to the Ottawa Little Theatre for the first time since it had become a travelling festival—just one year before he died, much honoured for his contribution to both the organizations he had served for so long.

9. *Love and Whisky* by Betty Lee, McClelland & Stewart, 1973, *op. cit.*, p. 79.
10. *Ibid.*, p. 93.
11. *Ibid.*, p. 115.
12. *Ibid.*, p. 185.

PHOTO: KARSH

The Dynamo!

Dorothy White
(1893-1965)

Theatre pioneer, administrator, actress, director, fundraiser and all-round tireless worker, Dorothy White was one of Ottawa Little Theatre's greatest strengths for most of her adult life.

"When one thinks of the Little Theatre, one thinks immediately of Dorothy White, for... Dorothy White *is* the Little Theatre," wrote William Cromarty, a former president of the group, in 1956.[13] He continues: "Her career with the Theatre in Ottawa, however, goes back much further than the Little Theatre. It begins at the time the Ottawa Drama League was presenting plays at the Russell Theatre, where her first role was that of a pretty and attractive nursemaid....At the formal opening of the Little Theatre, Dorothy White recited an ode of welcome and praise written by one of Canada's foremost poets, Duncan Campbell Scott, who at the time was President of the Drama League....[she] was one of the first of the amateur directors[14] [and] was also for some years the Secretary of the organization. Since that time, Dorothy has directed many plays, always in a distinguished manner. She won the Bessborough Trophy with a delightful presentation of *French Without Tears*[15] (by Terence Rattigan) and she has been the guide and friend of the Children's Theatre and of all the groups that have gone forward from Ottawa to the Regionals and Finals of the Dominion Drama Festival....Growing older gracefully, Dorothy White

13. Ottawa Little Theatre Newsletter, Vol. 1, No. 9, May 1956, p. 1.
14. In its early years, the Ottawa Drama League employed a professional director, Rupert Caplan.
15. Ottawa Little Theatre's first Dominion Drama Festival prizewinner, 1938.

is still a member of the Board of Directors of the Little Theatre, and of the Dominion Drama Festival and she...still radiates vital enthusiasm for the theatre."

Generally regarded as "the most efficient worker, who smooths out sundry difficulties,"[16] she was the gracious hostess to visiting competitors in the early years of the Dominion Drama Festival. She ran the theatre office, acted, directed and was one of the theatre's chief policy-makers.

As her sons Richard and Wallis put it: "Mother was a dynamo! Ottawa Little Theatre was very, very important to her." As she was to it. As "the heart of Ottawa's amateur dramatic movement, she was also 'in' most anything else for the good of the community...a woman interested in life, delighting to see the pretentious stuck with a hatpin, [living] wholly and [dealing] in happiness."[17]

A Fundraising Force
Elizabeth (Betty) Cruikshank (1882-1979)

This photograph was taken shortly after Elizabeth's engagement in 1905.

PHOTO: Courtesy of Miriam Lewis

The small girl clasped her father's hand tightly and looked wide-eyed around the Victoria Museum auditorium. She was just eight years old and she was very excited to be in the theatre. Her gaze swept from the heavy curtain hiding the stage to the people in their grand evening clothes. She tried hard to sit still while she waited for the play to begin. Then she would see her mother.

16. *Love and Whisky, op. cit.*, p. 115.
17. Obituary, *Ottawa Journal,* May 1965.

"My first memory of the Ottawa Drama League was being taken to the museum as a special treat to see Mother on stage," says Miriam Lewis. "I can still see myself going backstage in tears afterwards because she was so perfectly lovely."

Mariam Lewis—she was Mimsy Cruikshank then—was to see her mother, Elizabeth, cross the stage many times after that special outing in 1924 and was often with her when she was busy with other theatre-related activities.

As one of the League's stalwarts from its very early days, Elizabeth Cruikshank headed the fundraising campaign which enabled the League to buy its own building. "We used to sit in a miserable little office on Wellington Street during the bond drive," Mimsy says, recalling how $25 mortgage bonds were sold "person-to-person."

Then, as the fundraising campaign drew to a successful conclusion, League members turned their attention to equipping their theatre. "They had been told that Yale had the best lighting equipment for a small theatre," says Mariam Lewis. "So Mama and I went down to New Haven and went all through the beautiful little theatre at

Elizabeth Cruikshank and daughter Miriam.

PHOTO: KARSH

Yale. [On her recommendation] the same lighting panel was put into Ottawa Little Theatre."

Betty Cruikshank was a major force in the theatre's development from 1914, when she led the first play reading of Maxim Gorky's *In the Depths*—in response to a call from Madge Macbeth, then League president, for the establishment of a reading circle. In 1926, she chaired the fundraising committee for the new building. In 1970—then 87 years old—she was a strong supporter of the drive to rebuild after the great fire.

"Mother was beside herself the night of the fire," recalls Mimsy. "I was in Montreal when I heard on the (radio) news that the Ottawa Little Theatre was on fire. I called her right away and drove up to be with her. There she was, sitting straight up in bed, bound and determined that the theatre should be rebuilt. Early the next morning she called Jane Murray to say: 'You have to rebuild'."

Betty Cruikshank was there for the opening of the new theatre less than two years later and there again for every show until the day she died in 1979, at the age of 96. Ottawa Little Theatre had been an important part of her life since 1906, when she came to Ottawa as a young bride, and new Smith graduate.

Today, Mimsy Lewis and her husband, Daniel, occupy the theatre seats that had belonged to her parents for so many years. Surrounded by memories that reach back to Ottawa Little Theatre's beginnings, Mimsy recalls her days in the theatre's Junior League—memories of Dorothy White as an excellent director, but "a tough lady to work for," director Rupert Caplan as a person whom "you just wanted to please" and the excitement of escorting the Governor General to his seat.

"We (members of the Junior League) were the ticket takers," she says. "We wore uniforms then and used to usher everyone to their seats. Two would be chosen to greet the Governor General (and his party). That was the big thrill. We would stand at the entrance into the foyer and then walk them down the aisle. Then we would stand with our backs to the proscenium arch, curtsey and hand them their programs."

Almost seventy years later, such a ceremony is a distant memory, but the sense of continuity shines through with the passing of the seats in Row D from mother to daughter.

Mr. OLT

Bill Adkins (1889-1982)

The man who was Ottawa Little Theatre's resident stage manager for almost sixty years says, "I wasn't interested in theatre until...Dr. Duncan Campbell Scott (his boss at Indian Affairs) asked me to help him with a play."[18] That was in 1923, while the Ottawa Drama League was performing in the Russell Theatre—"a great big barn of a place, very ornate, but the stage was not too big," recalled Mr. Adkins,[19] (unlike the Ottawa Little Theatre's spacious stage, his tone suggests). Outside the Russell, coachmen waited in horse-drawn carriages to drive patrons home after the shows, he said.

What an interesting introduction to theatre that must have been for the World War I veteran, who joined the Department of Indian Affairs when the war was over. He quickly became fascinated with the workings of the stage, and when the Ottawa Drama League moved into its own theatre became its stage manager.

"In those days," he recalled, "everybody did everything. I did props, helped move the furniture—everything."[20] He continued doing (or supervising) "everything that mattered in theatre work" for the next half century and, in 1972, his tremendous contribution to theatre was recognized when he was made a member of the Order of Canada.

"No one will ever love a theatre the way Bill Adkins did," said Ottawa Little Theatre president Jane Murray after his death in 1982.[21]

"He seemed to have the solution to every impossible problem," says long-time member Kevin Conlon.

18. Taped interview with Grace Lydiatt Shaw, 1965, National Archives of Canada, *op. cit.*
19. *Ibid.*
20. "Bill Adkins Remembers Them All," *Ottawa Citizen*, *op. cit.*
21. Obituary, *Ottawa Citizen*, April 1982.

It might be making a piano. He and his crew once constructed an instrument in just one day for the production of *Nude With a Violin* by Noel Coward. It could be preparing a revolving stage for Lionel Bart's musical *Oliver*. (The revolve was operated manually with a winch and a rope.)

A behind-the-scenes genius who was "not fussy about getting before the public,"[22] he was the person who ensured that the show would go on. Few people could imagine Ottawa Little Theatre without Bill Adkins, known around the city as "Mr. OLT."

By 1953, he had taken early retirement from his public service job and moved into the theatre full-time. "I retired from my job as soon as I could because I was far more interested in the theatre," he says. "I had grown up with it. Something happens to you when you get attached to theatre." [23]

From then on, he spent very little time at his nearby apartment. He preferred his small room in the basement of the theatre. A similar domain, decorated with Karsh photographs and a few out-of-commission props, was recreated in the new theatre after the 1970 fire.

"You knew you had arrived at Ottawa Little Theatre when you were invited to Bill's room for a drink after a show," says Leonie Gardner. "I can still remember the first time Bill invited me in to join the group—the laughter, the fun, the jokes. I can't remember when I had so much fun."

PHOTO: Courtesy of *Ottawa Citizen*

Gracious Iron Lady

Jane Murray (1918-)

A framed cartoon graced the wall of Jane Murray's red-carpeted office in Ottawa Little Theatre in the 1960s. Presented to her by her children, it was a wry comment on the lack of home baking when mother was busy with amateur theatre. And busy she remained for more than thirty years, over twenty-five of them as president. Even after she retired from office in

22. "Bill Adkins Remembers Them All," *Ottawa Citizen, op. cit.*
23. Taped interview with Grace Lydiatt Shaw, *op. cit.*

1989, she was at the theatre to welcome patrons, always the gracious and elegant hostess greeting her guests as she handed out programs. In that simple gesture, she maintained the tone of gentility that had been the theatre's hallmark from its beginnings.

There was never any doubt about her love and commitment to her theatre; her immense contribution was officially recognized with an Order of Canada in 1978. Neither would anyone question her iron determination. She was at the helm when the theatre burned to the ground. She was one of the driving forces in raising the money to rebuild. Like Dorothy White before her, she *was* the spirit of Ottawa Little Theatre for many years. And like her predecessor, Duncan Campbell Scott, she expected to be obeyed—and almost always was.

"She usually got her way, but then, her way was usually the best route," says Charles Haines, a member of the board of directors at the time of the fire. "As chairman of the board, she was absolutely brilliant at running meetings and she ran a very tight ship."

"Jane Murray can be a formidable opponent...but there is a great deal of warmth underneath that...uncompromising manner, and a determination that commands respect. She really loves that theatre, and she defends it and protects it like a mother hen with her chicks," wrote Audrey Ashley in 1978.[24]

For many years, Jane Murray selected the plays and chose the directors. Though her selections were presented to a play-reading committee and the full board of directors, its members rarely disagreed with her. Her objective was to please the audience. Her choices were generally commercially shrewd. Her answer to any criticism was to point to the theatre's success, particularly after she instituted the play-per-month schedule—a move that increased Ottawa Little Theatre's already high profile.

Ready to battle City Hall whenever necessary, always a staunch defender of the theatre she loved, Jane Murray continued Ottawa Little Theatre's proud traditions as well as leaving her personal stamp on the institution that she ran for more than a quarter of a century

24. "50 Years of Love—Little Theatre Grows Through Fire," *Ottawa Citizen, op. cit.*

CHAPTER 8

The Play's the Thing

Young and old come forth to play.
John Milton
in *L'Allegro*

Nobody, but nobody, does things the way we do at Ottawa Little Theatre.
Val Bogan
Board member, 1997

In 1997, the days of just one person being the hub of the theatre operation have passed. As Ottawa Little Theatre has grown with the city, it has become less of a club, more of a well-oiled machine focused on the business of presenting plays.

"Part of the joy of the theatre today is that it runs so smoothly," says current board president Sybil Cooke. "That is because we have a very hard-working and efficient staff and a working board (with specified responsibilities)."

Most of the time, one play is on the boards, a second is in rehearsal, and a director is auditioning actors for a third. Regular adult and junior drama classes are in session. Registrations are being accepted for special events—a workshop headed by a well-known actor such as R.H. Thomson or a trip to the Stratford Festival led by Sybil Cooke, perhaps. Downstairs in the workshops, sets are under construction. Costumes are being designed, fitted and sewn. (At the same time, others from the hundreds in stock are being rented out, an increasingly busy part of the costume department's daily work.) Upstairs, the box office telephone rings almost constantly. The photographer delivers shots of the next production. The program is sent out for printing. A patron drops in to buy a ticket. In the board room, the next season's subscription campaign is in full swing.

Sybil Cooke, Ottawa Little Theatre president since 1990, standing outside the theatre.
PHOTO: Lynn Ball, *Ottawa Citizen*

"This place lives and breathes 365 days a year," says board member Jim Bishop. His particular assignment is to watch over the front of house. These days, he is usually one of the people beaming the greeting to patrons and handing out programs—around ten thousand of them for each show.

"I'm so proud when I go by and see all those bodies going into the theatre or glance up and see the crowds by the windows and around the bar during intermission," says Kenneth Binks, the man who headed the rebuilding campaign and a subscriber for the last forty years. "Ottawa Little Theatre is still one of the most successful enterprises in Ottawa because it has never gone around with its hand out. It's an 85-year success story."

Much of that success is rooted in its long-established traditions. But, audiences will fill the seats only as long as they enjoy the plays, as Jane Murray regularly pointed out. So the first essential is to select a season of shows with popular appeal. That's how Helen Jerome's adaptation of Jane Austen's classic novel *Pride and Prejudice* came to be one of Ottawa Little Theatre's hits in 1997.

"We decided to do it before the end of 1995," says Sybil Cooke, who directed the production. "We have to have our program together by the October of one year to present to the board for approval. Then the season is printed in the January program of the following year and we start the membership drive for the next season."

The plays, selected by a play-reading committee, are a mix of styles within the tried-and-true parameters that Ottawa Little Theatre knows its audiences prefer. Practical considerations—such as avoiding juxtaposing two plays that require complex, multiple sets and ensuring that performing rights are available—also loom large in play choice. But, unlike professional theatres, Ottawa Little Theatre does not have to worry about the affordability of large-cast plays. (*Pride and Prejudice* has a cast of twenty-five.) This was always one of the arguments that Bill Adkins and Jane Murray advanced for retaining the amateur status of "the most well-loved theatre in the country...[where everyone] has a chance to go on stage."[1] It is even more relevant today.

"The committee has to be extremely careful and objective about choosing and grouping plays," says Sybil. "Members are not choosing a play because they particularly want to direct it or because it contains a part they particularly want to play. They are choosing a balance of plays that they think the audience will enjoy."

That can take a while. Eventually, selections made and approved, the play-reading committee has one more task: choosing the directors for each play. Once more, the board must give its nod of approval, before directors are approached.[2]

Sybil, a regular on the list of the theatre's directors as well as its president, was asked to direct *Pride and Prejudice* as far back as November 1995. That gave her time for production meetings with the set designer and backstage staff—quite apart from reading both play and novel again and again—before arranging auditions in February 1996. Even this apparently simple task requires careful orchestration.

"You have to do the auditions when a play is running so that the stage is available on Sundays," she says. "Otherwise, it's being used for rehearsals."

More than two hundred and fifty people responded to the audition call. Gradually, two or three sessions later, Sybil had seen every performer in action and had whittled the group down to a manageable forty. One more session, one more matching and culling of performers, and she was ready.

"I take a long time to cast," she says, "because it's the most important thing of all." She also takes a while to explain the extent of the commitment, a solid six weeks of rehearsing and performing. "I make sure that everyone understands this when they come into the play."

---

1. "'Wobbly Little Organization' Best-Loved Theatre in Country" by Charles Pope, *Scene Changes*, Vol. 4, No. 4, May/June 1976, p. 8.
2. Unlike many community theatre groups, directors are limited to accepting or refusing a particular play. They are not involved in the selection.

Program design of 1938 production of Jane Austen's *Pride and Prejudice,* adapted by Helene Jerome, directed by E.G. Sterndale Bennett.

The first rehearsal, a read-through of the script, is called for the following Sunday. "It has to be a Sunday because the play before is still in the rehearsal hall," she points out. As soon as the play ahead of it completes its run, it will finish rehearsals on the stage and *Pride and Prejudice* can move up the line into the rehearsal hall, three nights a week and Sunday afternoons. "But I don't believe in late (night) rehearsals," adds Sybil. "Most people have other jobs."

Sandwiched between rehearsals are regular production meetings and consultations with the set designer. "Robin (Riddihough) came up with an idea for the set (a backdrop of an enlargement of a 1785 engraving and minimal scene changes to keep the action flowing) that was exactly what I wanted," she says.

Francesca Ranalli, Margaret Shearman and Amy Rutherford in the 1997 production of Helene Jerome's adaptation of *Pride and Prejudice* by Jane Austen, directed by Sybil Cooke.
PHOTO: Michael Vuckovic

She converted the play from its original three acts to two, because "audiences don't tolerate three acts very well any more," and set about guiding her actors, refining timing and dealing with a multitude of technical details. "My work doesn't stop until opening night. Then it's up to the cast and crew. There's nothing for the director to do on opening night. I always feel like a spare piece watching a child leaving home."

But leave home it does, heralded by the National Anthem, as have hundreds of other Ottawa Little Theatre productions over the years. Then, as the lights dim and the theatre's crest above the stage glows in the darkness, the audience settles back into plush-covered comfort and the heavy, red velvet curtains are drawn back. There is a collective intake of breath, a sprinkling of hand-clapping in appreciation of the light charm of the set. A moment's pause and the play begins.

The preamble was probably very similar the last time Ottawa Little Theatre presented *Pride and Prejudice* in 1938, almost sixty years ago. "Was it really sixty years ago?" asks Bea Brace, the life member who coordinated the theatre's 75th anniversary cookbook. "I played Jane (the oldest daughter in the Bennett family) then, you know." And Dorothy White, the spirit of Ottawa Little Theatre for so many years, played Lady Catherine de Bourgh, while former president Michael Meiklejohn stage-managed the production. The link between past and present is strong as ever.

Epilogue

We can only pay our debt to the past by putting the future in debt to ourselves.
John Buchan, Lord Tweedsmuir
Governor General of Canada and
Ottawa Little Theatre Patron
1935-1940

Some of Ottawa Little Theatre's long history is evident as soon as you enter its doors. The one remaining pew from the church that became the original theatre still sits in the lower foyer. A bust of Sarah Bernhardt stands nearby. (Apparently she was forgiven for absconding with the tri-color that members of the Ottawa Drama League had borrowed to decorate her dressing room in the Russell Theatre.) At one side of the spacious upstairs foyer stands the imposing Pope's throne from the production of *Hadrian VII*, the inaugural show in the new theatre built after the great fire of 1970—now more than a quarter of a century old.

Hundreds of photographs bear witness to a long collective memory. The decoration on the programs, still noting the current Governor General as the Honorary Patron, is another thread between past and present. A newer, but now well established, tradition of displaying works of art in the red-carpeted foyer, coupled with the fireplace at one side and the well-stocked bar at the other, add to the sense of occasion. As always, the impression of warmth, welcome and, most of all, tradition contribute to the comfort level as the audience rounds the curve of the staircase.

There's a buzz of conversation as greetings are exchanged. Many of the people here have known each other for years. They may have been on stage for the last show or be involved with the next. Others have been Ottawa Little Theatre subscribers for so long, many of them coming on the same night and sitting in the same seats for each show, that they have simply built friendships with their neighbours.

This theatre is part of their personal tradition, their season tickets a family heirloom to be willed to their children.

Ottawa Little Theatre remains an important part of the lives of everyone who has acted or worked there. For that matter, it remains part of the core of theatre across the country. As the first home of the Dominion Drama Festival, it had a tremendous influence on the developing Canadian theatrical scene. Through its playwriting competition, it continues to support new Canadian drama. Through its alumni, it flourishes on professional and community theatre stages in other parts of the country and beyond our national borders. And in Ottawa, this most professional amateur theatre continues staging a legend that shows every sign of continuing into the distant future.

APPENDIX I

Key Dates

1913
(May 9) Society for the Study and Production of Dramatic Art founded.

1913
(November 15) The Society, now called the Ottawa Drama League, presents its first show, an evening of one-act plays at thc Russell Theatre.

1915
Ottawa Drama League moves to the Victoria Memorial Museum auditorium.

1916
The League presents *The Suffragist* by Donald Guthrie. A Canadian play by an Ottawa playwright, performed by local actors, it was considered a landmark in Canadian theatrical development.

1916
Fire destroys the Parliament buildings. House of Commons moves to the museum until they are rebuilt and the Ottawa Drama League loses its theatre.

1923
The League returns to the museum theatre.

1928
(January 3) The official opening of Ottawa Little Theatre, the League's own building.

1931
Lord Bessborough becomes Governor General of Canada.

1933
Dominion Drama Festival founded. Ottawa Little Theatre hosts the festival for its first five years.

1936
The League founds its Workshop to perform experimental plays and administer a

one-act playwriting competition to encourage Canadian drama and present the winning plays. Although the Workshop had ended by 1960, the playwriting competition continues.

1938
Ottawa Drama League wins the Bessborough Trophy at the Dominion Drama Festival with its production of *French Without Tears* by Terence Rattigan, directed by Dorothy White.

1940
The League rents out the theatre as a movie house during the war years. It still presents plays there on Sundays and retains the use of the basement.

1947
The League regains full use of the theatre.

1948
The Dominion Drama Festival returns to Ottawa Little Theatre for the first time since becoming a travelling festival.

1949
Ottawa Drama League presents Robertson Davies' *Eros at Breakfast* at the Edinburgh Drama Festival.

1951
The League changes its name to Ottawa Little Theatre.

1960
Following the closure of the Workshop, the 71-seat Theatre Under the Stairs is created in the basement of Ottawa Little Theatre.

1963
Ottawa Little Theatre celebrates its 50th birthday with a Golden Anniversary tea. A number of the original members attend.

1969
Ottawa Little Theatre is renovated.

1969
The National Arts Centre opens.

1970
Ottawa Little Theatre burns to the ground.

1972
The new theatre opens. The first production is Peter Luke's *Hadrian VII.*

1977
Ottawa Little Theatre pays off the mortgage on its building. It has remained debt-free ever since.

1982
Ottawa Little Theatre celebrates its 10th anniversary in the new theatre by commissioning playwright/public servant Chris Burke to write *Don't Despair, Fonctionnaire*, a satire about life in the public service.

1988
Ottawa Little Theatre celebrates its 75th anniversary. It commemorates the occasion by publishing a celebrity cookbook.

1997
Ottawa Little Theatre celebrates 25 years in its "new" theatre.

APPENDIX II

Play List

Editor's note: Every effort has been made to make this list of plays accurate and exhaustive. However, because the Ottawa Drama League did not own a theatre until 1928 and did not always include play lists in its minutes, some productions may have been omitted. Many of the early productions were one-act plays. For some, no record of the authors was uncovered.

1913

Magic	G.K. Chesterton
The Dear Departed	Stanley Houghton
Riders to the Sea	John Synge

1914

In the early days, lectures, play study and social events were the Ottawa Drama League's primary focus. Then "Madge Macbeth called for reading circles as educational centres"—minutes, September 21.

The first play reading was led by Elizabeth Cruikshank:

In the Depths	Maxim Gorky

1915-1916

The Suffragist	Donald Guthrie
The Honeymoon	Arnold Bennett
Behind the Beyond (adapted by Jack Randall Crawford)	Stephen Leacock
Why the Chimes Rang	Elizabeth McFadden
Master Will of Stratford	Collective?

(presented to celebrate the tercentenary of Shakespeare's birth)

1916-1917

Proceeds from performances of one-act plays went to help the war effort.

The Tyranny of Tears
Holly Tree Inn
The Baby Blue Dog

The Ring	
Mrs. Mainwaring's Management	
The Rose and the Ring	
The Mollusc	H.H. Davies

1917-1918

A Christmas Carol (scenes)	Charles Dickens

Single performances for private groups

The Marriage of Kitty	
His House in Order	Sir Arthur Wing Pinero

1918-1919

A Single Man	H.H. Davies
Alice-sit-by-the-fire	J.M. Barrie

1919-1920

The Cassilis Engagement	St. John Hankin

1920-1921

His House in Order	Sir Arthur Wing Pinero

1921-1922

The Silver Box	John Galsworthy
The Point of View	Marian Osborne
The Lost Silk Hat	Lord Dunsany
The Twelve Pound Look	J.M. Barrie
Suppressed Desires	Susan Claspell

1922-1923

The Show Shop	James Forbes
The Truth	Clyde Fritch
The Man Who Married a Dumb Wife	
A Kiss in the Dark	Victor Herbert (music) & Marian Osborne
Wurzel Flummery	A.A. Milne
Mr. Pim Passes By	A.A. Milne
Augustus Does His Bit	George Bernard Shaw

1923-1924

Followers	Harold Brighouse
The Monkey's Paw (from the short story by W.W. Jacobs)	Louis N. Parker
The Two Mr. Wetherbys	St. John Hankin

The Romantic Age	A.A. Milne
The Maker of Dreams	
Lonesomelike	
An Offering to Brahma	Samuel Wilson
Everybody's Husband	Gilbert Cannon
In the Zone	Eugene O'Neil
Rosalind	J.M. Barrie

1924-1925

You Never Can Tell	George Bernard Shaw
The First Year	Frank Craven
Candida	George Bernard Shaw
Low Life	Mazo de la Roche
Matmata	Lawrence Langner
The Old Lady Shows Her Medals	J. M. Barrie

1925-1926

Hay Fever	Noel Coward
Outward Bound	Sutton Vane
The Admiral	
Aren't We All	Frederick Lonsdale
The Pigeon	John Galsworthy
Captain Applejack	
The Show Off	George Kelly
Chitra	Rabinranath Tagore
Augustus in Search of a Father	Harold Chaplin
The Maker of Dreams	Oliphant Down

1926-1927

Arms and the Man	George Bernard Shaw
Sun Up	Lula Vollmer
The Last of Mrs. Cheyney	Frederick Lonsdale

1927-1928

Anthony and Anna	St. John Ervine
Loyalties	John Galsworthy
Mary the Third	Rachel Crothers
The Romantic Young Lady	G. Martinez Sierra translated by Helen & Harley Granville-Barker
Dear Brutus	James Barrie

1928-1929

The Devil in the Cheese	Tom Cushing

A Bill of Divorcement	Clemence Dane
The Dover Road	A.A. Milne
R.U.R.	Karel Capek
What Every Woman Knows	J.M. Barrie
The Queen's Husband	R.E. Sherwood

1929-1930

Cock Robin	Elmer Rice & Philip Barry
Pygmalion	George Bernard Shaw
I'll Leave it to You	Noel Coward
Outward Bound	Sutton Vane
The First Mrs. Fraser	St. John Ervine
Bird-in-Hand	John Drinkwater

1930-1931

The Devil's Disciple	George Bernard Shaw
By Candle Light (adapted from the German by Harry Graham)	Siegfried Geyer
Saturday's Children	Maxwell Anderson
The Circle	Somerset Maugham
Expressing Willie	Rachel Crothers

1931-1932

Interference	Roland Pertwee & Harold Dearden
The Cat and the Cherub	C.B. Fernald
The Truth About Blayds	A.A. Milne
The Middle Watch	Ian Hay & Stephen King-Hall
Hamlet (touring production by Montreal Repertory Company)	William Shakespeare
The Swan	Ferenc Molnar
The Young Idea	Noel Coward
Dulcy	George S. Kaufman & Marc Connelly
Canaries Sometimes Sing	Frederick Lonsdale

1932-1933

There's Always Juliet	John Van Druten
The Cradle Song (translated by John Garrett Underhill)	G. Martinez Sierra
Bound East for Cardiff	Eugene O'Neill
The Crime at Blossoms	Mordaunt Shairp
Mrs. Moonlight	Benn W. Levy

On Approval	Frederick Lonsdale
1933-1934	
And So To Bed	J.B. Fagan
Mr. Prohack	Arnold Bennett & Edward Knoblock
Romeo and Juliet	William Shakespeare
The Skin Game	John Galsworthy
See Naples and Die	Elmer Rice
As Husbands Go	Rachel Crothers
1934-1935	
The Late Christopher Bean	Sidney Bean
On the Spot	Edgar Wallace
Tobias and the Angel	James Bridie
When Ladies Meet	Rachel Crothers
Elizabeth the Queen	Maxwell Anderson
1935-1936	
Post Road	Wilbur Steele & Norma Mitchell
Escape	John Galsworthy
Her Master's Voice	Clare Kummer
Captain Brassbound's Conversion	George Bernard Shaw
HMS Pinafore (with Orpheus Operatic Society)	W.S. Gilbert & Arthur Sullivan
1936-1937	
The Pirates of Penzance (with Orpheus Operatic Society)	W.S. Gilbert & Arthur Sullivan
Laburnum Grove	J.B. Priestley
St. Joan	George Bernard Shaw
The Wind and the Rain	Merton Hodge
Street Scene	Elmer Rice
Nine till Six	Aimee & Philip Stuart
First Lady	Katharine Dayton & George S. Kaufman
1937-1938	
Private Lives	Noel Coward
Mary of Scotland	Maxwell Anderson
Pride and Prejudice (adapted from the novel by Jane Austen)	Helen Jerome
Judgment Day	Elmer Rice
The Petrified Forest	Robert Emmet Sherwood

Ladies of Creation	Gladys Unger
1938-1939	
Libel	Edward Wooll
French Without Tears	Terence Rattigan
Tovarich (adapted by Robert E. Sherwood)	Jacques Deval
Stage Door	Edna & Robert E. Ferber & George S. Kaufman
1939-1940	
Spring Meeting	M.J. Farrell & John Perry
Kind Lady	Edward Chodorov
Ah, Wilderness	Eugene O'Neill
Dear Octopus	Dodie Smith
You Can't Take It With You	Moss Hart & George S. Kaufman
1940-1941	
Tony Draws a Horse	Lesley Storm
Our Town	Thornton Wilder
1941-1942	
Ottawa Little Theatre Revue	
High Tor	Maxwell Anderson
The Time of Your Life	William Saroyan
1942-1943	
Arsenic and Old Lace	J.O. Kesselring
My Sister Eileen	Joseph Fields & Jerome Chodorov
Orders is Orders	Ian Hay & Anthony Armstrong
The Male Animal	James Thurber & Elliot Nugent
1943-1944	
The Wingless Victory	Maxwell Anderson
When We Are Married	J.B. Priestley
Dark Eyes	Eugenie Leontovich & Elena Miramova
1944-1945	
The Torch Bearers	George Kelly
Theatre	Guy Bolton & Somerset Maugham
Claudia	Rose Franken
Tomorrow the World	James Gow & Armand D'Usseau
Fanny and the Servant Problem	Jerome K. Jerome

The Little Foxes	Lillian Hellman
Murder in a Nunnery	Emmet Lavery

1945-1946

The White Steed	Paul Vincent Carroll
Peer Gynt	Henrik Ibsen
Jacobowsky and the Colonel	S.N. Berhman
My Life with Caroline	
Resurrection	
Mr. and Mrs. North	Owen Davis
Maytime	
SNAFU	Louis Solomon & Harold Buchman
Papa Is All	Patterson Greene

1946-1947

The Gentle People	Irwin Shaw
Blithe Spirit	Noel Coward
Guest in the House	Hagar Wilde & Dale Eunson
Joan of Lorraine	Maxwell Anderson
Abraham and Isaac	Anonymous
The Full Moon	Hall Spence
His First Date	James Reach
Still Life	Noel Coward
Dark Brown	Philip Johnson
Five at "The George"	Stuart Ready
The House with the Twisty Windows	Mary Packington

1947-1948

The Great Big Doorstep	Frances Goodrich & Albert Hackett
Uncle Harry	Thomas Job
The Crystal Garden	Hugh Parker
The Cherry Orchard	Anton Chekhov
The Circle	Somerset Maugham
Man of Destiny	George Bernard Shaw
Murder at the Embassy	Hugh Parker
The Wandering Scholar	Hans Sachs
Family Album	Noel Coward
Merry Molly Malone	Brian McCarthy
Molly and Me	Margot Belier
Dear Ruth	Norman Krasna

1948-1949

Night Must Fall	Emlyn Williams

Fortune My Foe	Robertson Davies
Aladdin & the Wonderful Lamp	William Doyle
The Stolen Prince	Dan Totheroh
I Remember Mama	John Van Druten
All My Sons	Arthur Miller
Arms and the Man	George Bernard Shaw

1949-1950

Boy Meets Girl	Bella & Samuel Spewack
There Goes Yesterday	Murray Davis
The Emperor's New Clothes	
The Two Mrs. Carrolls	Martin Vale
The Winslow Boy	Terence Rattigan
Another Part of the Forest	Lillian Hellman
Charley's Aunt	Brandon Thomas
Come-By-Chance	Graham McInnes

1950-1951

The Road to Rome	Robert Emmet Sherwood
Life With Mother	Howard Lindsay & Russell Crouse
Danbury Fair	Albert Carriere
A Phoenix Too Frequent	Christopher Fry
Therese	Thomas Job
Argus Bank	Graham Ferguson
Kiss and Tell	F. Hugh Herbert
The Last Best West	Graham McInnes & Norman Gilchrist
Pinocchio	
The Pirate's Daughter	
Rip Van Winkle	

1951-1952

The Late George Apley	John P. Marquand & George S. Kaufman
Candida	George Bernard Shaw
Edward, My Son	Robert Morley & Noel Langley
Gramercy Ghost	John Cecil Holm
A Streetcar Named Desire	Tennessee Williams
Sabrina Fair	Samuel Taylor
The Silver Whistle	Robert E. McEnroe

1952-1953

The Happy Time	Samuel Taylor
The Play's the Thing	Ferenc Molnar

The Madwoman of Chaillot	Jean Giraudoux
The Merry Wives of Windsor	William Shakespeare
Bell, Book and Candle	John Van Druten
The Enchanted	Jean Giraudoux
Elizabeth the Queen	Maxwell Anderson
Riders to the Sea	John Synge
When Shakespeare's Ladies Meet	Charles George
How He Lied to Her Husband	George Bernard Shaw

1953-1954

Our Hearts were Young and Gay	Jean Kerr
Amphitryon 38	Jean Giraudoux
Ring Around the Moon	Jean Anouilh
The Innocents (based on Henry James' *The Turn of the Screw)*	William Archibald
Private Lives	Noel Coward
Detective Story	Sidney Kingsley
Gigi (from the novel by Colette)	Anita Loos

1954-1955

My Three Angels	Sam & Bella Spewack
The Moon in the Yellow River	Denis Johnston
Father of the Bride (based on the novel by Edward Streeter)	Caroline Francke
Dangerous Corner	J.B. Priestley
A Phoenix Too Frequent	Christopher Fry
Androcles and the Lion	George Bernard Shaw
East Lynne	Ned Albert
Stars in our Eyes	Jack McCreath
Love in Idleness	Terence Rattigan

1955-1956

When We Are Married	J.B. Priestley
The Crucible	Arthur Miller
The Importance of Being Earnest	Oscar Wilde
Old Acquaintance	John Van Druten
The Women	Clare Boothe Luce
The Caine Mutiny Court Martial	Herman Wouk
Gruach	Gordon Bottomley
Helena's Husband	Philip Moeller
Broadway	Philip Dunning & George Abbott

1956-1957

The Tender Trap	Max Shulman & Robert Paul Smith
Pygmalion	George Bernard Shaw
Teach Me How to Cry	Patricia Joudry
Robin Hood	James Norris
The Remarkable Mr Pennypacker	Liam O'Brian
Barefoot in Athens	Maxwell Anderson
Anastasia	Marcelle Maurette
The Happy Breed	Noel Coward
Thieves' Carnival	Jean Anouilh
The Solid Gold Cadillac	Howard Teichmann & George S. Kaufman

1957-1958

The Desperate Hours	Joseph Hayes
The Grass Harp	Truman Capote
The Teahouse of the August Man	John Patrick
Encounter at the Brink	William Digby
Voices of Desire	Edwin R. Procunier
Zanorin	Catherine Brickenden
The Chalk Garden	Enid Bagnold
The Lark	Jean Anouilh
Witness for the Prosecution	Agatha Christie
Tiger at the Gates	Jean Giraudoux
Light Up the Sky	Moss Hart
Season in the Sun	Wolcott Gibbs

1958-1959

Visit to a Small Planet	Gore Vidal
The Love of Four Colonels	Peter Ustinov
The Reluctant Debutante	William Douglas Home
Dark of the Moon	Howard Richardson & William Berney
The Mousetrap	Agatha Christie
Waltz of the Toreadors	Jean Anouilh
Lo and Behold	John Patrick
Separate Tables	Terence Rattigan

1959-1960

The Sleeping Prince	Terence Rattigan
The Matchmaker	Thornton Wilder
Nude with Violin	Noel Coward
The Potting Shed	Graham Greene

Bus Stop	William Inge
The Hollow	Agatha Christie
The Diary of Anne Frank	Frances Goodrich & Albert Hackett
Romanoff and Juliet	Peter Ustinov

1960-1961

The Seven Year Itch	George Axelrod
Ondine	Jean Giraudoux
Once More with Feeling	Harry Kurnitz
The Living Room	Graham Greene
Picnic	William Inge
Anne of the Thousand Days	Maxwell Anderson
The Happiest Millionaire	Kyle Crichton
Summer of the Seventeenth Doll	Ray Lawler

1961-1962

Wonderful Town	Joseph Fields & Jerome Chodorov
The Pleasure of his Company	Samuel Taylor
Look Back in Anger	John Osborne
Five Finger Exercise	Peter Shaffer
The Unexpected Guest	Agatha Christie
The Dark at the Top of the Stairs	William Inge
Send Me No Flowers	Norman Barasch & Carroll Moore
Under the Sycamore Tree	Samuel Spewack

1962-1963

Take Me Along (based on Eugene O'Neill's *Ah, Wilderness*)	Joseph Stein & Robert Russell, music by Robert Merrill
Toys in the Attic	Lillian Hellman
Dead on Nine	Jack Popplewell
The Complaisant Lover	Graham Greene
A Button Missing	George Blackburn
Of Mice and Men	John Steinbeck
Critic's Choice	Ira Levin
J.B.	Archibald MacLeish

1963-1964

Anything Goes	Guy Bolton, P.G. Wodehouse, Howard Lindsay, Russell Crouse & Cole Porter

A Taste of Honey	Shelagh Delaney
Write Me a Murder	Frederick Knott
Bousille and the Just	Gratien Gelinas
Marriage-go-round	Leslie Stevens
Rashomon	Fay & Michael Kanin
A Thurber Carnival	James Thurber
An Ideal Husband	Oscar Wilde
1964-1965	
Irma la Douce	Julian More, David Heneker, Monty Norman & Marguerite Monnot
The Miracle Worker	William Gibson
The Sound of Murder	William Fairchild
Tobacco Road	Jack Kirkland
La Ronde (adapted by Eric Bentley)	Arthur Schnitzler
Royal Gambit	Hermann Gressieker
Come Blow Your Horn	Neil Simon
Lady Windermere's Fan	Oscar Wilde
1965-1966	
Kiss Me Kate	Cole Porter, Sam & Bella Spewack
Long Day's Journey into Night	Eugene O'Neill
Sunday in New York	Norman Krasna
Present Laughter	Noel Coward
Never Too Late	Sumner Arthur Long
Gaslight	Patrick Hamilton
Epitaph for George Dillon	John Osborne & Anthony Creighton
The Inspector General	Nikolai Gogol
1966-1967	
Annie Get Your Gun	Irving Berlin, Dorothy & Herbert Fields
The Private Ear and the Public Eye	Peter Shaffer
You Can't Take it with You	Moss Hart & George S. Kaufman
The Centennial Play	Robertson Davies, W.O. Mitchell, Arthur Murphy & Yves Theriault
Becket	Jean Anouilh
Poor Richard	Jean Kerr
Dylan	Sydney Michaels

Good Morning, Mr. Bell	David Morley
Any Wednesday	Muriel Resnik

1967-1968

Oliver!	Lionel Bart
Hostile Witness	Jack Roffey
The Absence of a Cello	Ira Wallach
The Dance of Death	August Strindberg
Generation	William Goodhart
The Right Honourable Gentleman	Michael Dyne
Luther	John Osborne
How to Succeed in Business Without Really Trying	Frank Loesser, Abe Burrows, Jack Weinstock & Willie Gilbert

1968-1969

The Absence of a Cello	Ira Wallach
Camelot	Alan Jay Lerner & Frederick Loewe
The Elder Statesman	T.S. Eliot
Catch Me If You Can	Jack Weinstock & Willie Gilbert
The Caretaker	Harold Pinter
Say Who You Are	Keith Waterhouse & Willis Hall
The Three Sisters	Anton Chekhov
Holiday for Lovers	Ronald Alexander
The Fantastiks	Tom Jones & Harvey L. Schmidt

1969-1970

Gypsy	Arthur Laurents, Jule Styne & Stephen Sondheim
A Case of Libel	Henry Denker
Charley's Aunt	Brandon Thomas
Wait Until Dark	Frederick Knott
The Promise	Aleksei Arbuzov
The Loud Red Patrick	John Boruff
The Paisley Convertible	Harry Cauley
Stop the World, I Want to Get Off	Anthony Newley & Leslie Bricusse

1970-1971

The Price	Arthur Miller
Barefoot in the Park	Neil Simon
The Man in the Glass Booth	Robert Shaw
Exit the Body	Fred Carmichael

Harvey	Mary Chase
Half a Sixpence	Beverley Cross & David Heneker
Don't Drink the Water	Woody Allen
Halfway Up the Tree	Peter Ustinov

1971-1972

A Shot in the Dark	Michael Achard
On Monday Next	Philip King
Hadrian the Seventh	Peter Luke
Life with Father	Howard Lindsay & Russell Crouse
Middle of the Night	Paddy Chayefsky
The Star Spangled Girl	Neil Simon
Any Number Can Die	Fred Carmichael

1972-1973

Plaza Suite	Neil Simon
In the Matter of J. Robert Oppenheimer	Heinar Kipphardt
Forty Carats	Jay Allen
Butterflies are Free	Leonard Gershe
The Barretts of Wimpole Street	Hugh Besier
Relatively Speaking	Alan Ayckbourn
Masterpiece	Larry Ward & Gordon Russell
Play It Again, Sam	Woody Allen
The Secretary Bird	William Douglas Home
The Gazebo	Alec Coppel

1973-1974

Last of the Red Hot Lovers	Neil Simon
The Heiress	Ruth and Augustus Goetz
How the Other Half Loves	Alan Ayckbourn
Vivat! Vivat! Regina!	Robert Bolt
Night Watch	Lucille Fletcher
The Patrick Pearse Motel	Hugh Leonard
There's a Girl in my Soup	Terence Frisby
Chase Me, Comrade	Ray Cooney
The Odd Couple	Neil Simon
Ten Little Indians	Agatha Christie
The Time of the Cuckoo	Arthur Laurents

1974-1975

The Jockey Club Stakes	William Douglas Home

An Inspector Calls	J.B. Priestley
All For Mary	Harold Brooke & Kay Bannerman
According to the Evidence	Felicity Douglas & Henry Cecil
An Enemy of the People	Henrik Ibsen
The Brides of March	John Chapman
The Late Christopher Bean	Sidney Howard
The Mousetrap	Agatha Christie
Arsenic and Old Lace	Joseph Kesselring
Blithe Spirit	Noel Coward
The Pleasure of His Company	Samuel Taylor

1975-1976

The Prisoner of Second Avenue	Neil Simon
Prescription Murder	William Link & Richard Levinson
A Thousand Clowns	Herb Gardner
The Oblast Court Trial	Frank Daley
The Aspern Papers	Henry James & Michael Redgrave
Six Characters in Search of an Author	Luigi Pirandello
No Sex Please, We're British	Anthony Marriott & Alistair Foot
The Sunshine Boys	Neil Simon
Spider's Web	Agatha Christie
The Solid Gold Cadillac	Howard Techmann & George S. Kaufman

1976-1977

The Man of La Mancha	Dale Wasserman
Dial "M" for Murder	Frederick Knott
The Desk Set	William Marchant
The Lion in Winter	James Goldman
My Daughter, Your Son	Phoebe & Henry Ephron
The Madwoman of Chaillot	Jean Giraudoux
Move Over Mrs. Markham	Ray Cooney & John Chapman
6 RMS RIV VU	Bob Randall
Murder at the Vicarage	Agatha Christie
Best of Friends	James Elward

1977-1978

The Roar of the Greaspaint, The Smell of the Crowd	Anthony Newley & Leslie Bricusse
Anatomy of a Murder	Elihu Winer
The Late George Apley	John P. Marquand & George S. Kaufman

A Man for All Seasons	Robert Bolt
Not Now, Darling	Ray Cooney & John Chapman
The Day After the Fair	Frank Harvey
The Admirable Crichton	J.M. Barrie
Last of the Class	Fred Carmichael
Towards Zero	Agatha Christie
Big Bad Mouse	Philip King & Falkland L. Cary

1978-1979

A Funny Thing Happened on the Way to the Forum	Burt Shevelove, Larry Gelbart & Stephen Sondheim
Laburnum Grove	J.B. Priestley
Table Manners	Alan Ayckbourn
Ladies in Retirement	Edward Percy & Reginald Denham
Finishing Touches	Jean Kerr
Edward, My Son	Robert Morley & Noel Langley
See How They Run	Philip King
Living Together	Alan Ayckbourn
The Unexpected Guest	Agatha Christie
Come Blow Your Horn	Neil Simon
The Mousetrap	Agatha Christie

1979-1980

Cactus Flower	Abe Burrows
Night Must Fall	Emlyn Williams
Alphabetical Order	Michael Frayn
Glasstown	Noel Robinson
Children	A.R. Gurney
The Case in Question	Ronald Millar
Boeing-Boeing	Marc Camoletti
Love from a Stranger	Frank Vosper
The Man Who Came to Dinner	Moss Hart & George S. Kaufman
Charley's Aunt	Brandon Thomas

1980-1981

Chapter Two	Neil Simon
Roots	Arnold Wesker
Roar Like a Dove	Leslie Storm
King of Hearts	Jean Kerr & Eleanor Brooks
Elizabeth the Queen	Maxwell Anderson
There Goes the Bride	Ray Cooney & John Chapman
Rookery Nook	Ben Travers
A Murder is Announced	Agatha Christie
Third Best Sport	Leo & Eleanor Bayer

1981-1982

Rain	John Colton & Clemence Randolph
Da	Hugh Leonard
Summer and Smoke	Tennessee Williams
Cocktails with Mimi	Mary Chase
Suite in Two Keys	Noel Coward
Don't Despair, Fonctionnaire	Chris Burke
Cause Celebre	Terence Rattigan
13 Rue de l'Amour	Georges Feydeau
Octagon (adapted by Roy Haysden-Hinsley)	Guy de Maupassant
Witness for the Prosecution	Agatha Christie

1982-1983

I Ought to be in Pictures	Neil Simon
The Little Foxes	Lillian Hellman
A Christmas Carol (adapted by Chris Burke)	Charles Dickens
A Month in the Country	Ivan Turgenev
Ten Times Table	Alan Ayckbourn
Whose Life Is It Anyway?	Brian Clark
Happy Birthday	Marc Camoletti
The Philadelphia Story	Philip Barry
Deathtrap	Ira Levin
On Golden Pond	Ernest Thompson

1983-1984

The Machinery of Government	Chris Burke
My Cousin Rachel	Diana Morgan
My Three Angels	Sam & Bella Spewack
Talley's Folly	Lanford Wilson
Seven Keys to Baldpate	George M. Cohen
All My Sons	Arthur Miller
Pajama Tops	Jean De Letraz, Mawby Green & Ed Feilbert
Bedroom Farce	Alan Ayckbourn
The Prime of Miss Jean Brodie	Jay Presson Allen
Murder on the Nile	Agatha Christie

1984-1985

Mornings at Seven	Paul Osborn
The Dresser	Ronald Harwood
Barefoot in the Park	Neil Simon
Major Barbara	George Bernard Shaw

High Ground	Charlotte Hastings
A Streetcar Named Desire	Tennessee Williams
Who's Who?	Keith Waterhouse & Willis Hall
Dry Rot	John Chapman
The Butler Did It	Peter & Walter Marks
Children's Day	Keith Waterhouse & Willis Hall
1985-1986	
Educating Rita	Willy Russell
Quartermaine's Terms	Simon Gray
The Rape of the Belt	Benn W. Levy
Tartuffe	Moliere
The Children's Hour	Lillian Hellman
The Merchant	Arnold Wesker
Two Blind Mice	Samuel Spewack
Springtime for Henry	Benn W. Levy
Any Wednesday	Muriel Resnik
Black Coffee	Agatha Christie
1986-1987	
First Monday in October	Jerome Lawrence & Robert Lee
Pack of Lies	Hugh Whitemore
Harvey	Mary Chase
Mrs. Warren's Profession	George Bernard Shaw
I'll Be Back Before Midnight	Peter Colley
The Glass Menagerie	Tennessee Williams
The Au Pair Man	Hugh Leonard
The Odd Couple	Neil Simon
Pools Paradise	Philip King
Ten Little Indians	Agatha Christie
1987-1988	
Pardon Me, Prime Minister	Edward Taylor & John Graham
The Foreigner	Larry Shue
Silent Night, Lonely Night	Robert Anderson
Amadeus	Peter Shaffer
Murder by the Book	Duncan Greenwood & Robert King
The Crucible	Arthur Miller
My Friend Miss Flint	Donald Churchill & Peter Yeldhan
Plaza Suite	Neil Simon
The Remarkable Mr Pennypacker	Liam O'Brian
1988-1989	
The Sunshine Boys	Neil Simon

The Day They Kidnapped the Pope	Joao Bethencourt
Three Men on a Horse	George Abbott & John Cecil Holm
Jane Eyre (from the novel by Charlotte Bronte)	Helen Jerome
Not in the Book	Arthur Watkyn
Frankenstein (from the novel by Mary Shelley)	Tim Kelly
Alone Together	Lawrence Roman
A Midsummer Night's Dream	William Shakespeare
One for the Road	Willy Russell
Appointment with Death	Agatha Christie

1989-1990

The Nerd	Larry Shue
Caught in the Act	Trevor Cowper
The Man Who Came to Dinner	Moss Hart & George S. Kaufman
The Voysey Inheritance	Harley Granville-Barker
The Mark of Cain	Peter Colley
Twelve Angry Jurors	Reginald Rose
Social Security	Andrew Bergman
The Loud Red Patrick	John Boruff
The Thirteenth Chair	Bayard Vieillier

1990-1991

Broadway Bound	Neil Simon
Dead Ringer	Charles Ross
Stalag 17	Donald Bevan & Edmund Trzcinski
Wuthering Heights (from the novel by Emily Bronte)	Randolph Carter
Beyond Reasonable Doubt	Jeffrey Archer
Foxfire	Susan Cooper & Hume Cronyn
Two Into One	Ray Cooney
Don't Drink the Water	Woody Allen
Buterflies Are Free	Leonard Gershe
Murder at the Vicarage	Agatha Christie

1991-1992

Born Yesterday	Garson Kanin
Something to Hide	Leslie Sands
Steel Magnolias	Robert Harling
An Enemy of the People	Henrik Ibsen
Salesmen Don't Ride Bicycles	Leo Orenstein

Rebecca	Daphne Du Maurier
The Cocktail Hour	A.R. Gurney
Uproar in the House	Alistair Foot & Anthony Marriott
Enter Laughing	Joseph Stein
Spider's Web	Agatha Christie

1992-1993

Stepping Out	Richard Harris
A Few Good Men	Aaron Sorkin
Greetings	Tom Dudzick
The Importance of Being Earnest	Oscar Wilde
The Government Inspector	Nikolai Gogol
Emerald City	David Williamson
Rumors	Neil Simon
I Take this Man	Jack Sharkey
A Murder is Announced	Agatha Christie

1993-1994

The Odd Couple (Female)	Neil Simon
To Grandmother's House We Go	Joanna McClelland Glass
A Christmas Carol (adapted by Chris Burke)	Charles Dickens
The Cherry Orchard	Anton Chekhov
Murder Among Friends	Bob Barry
The Royal Baccarat Scandal	Royce Ryton
Other People's Money	Jerry Sterner
It Runs in the Family	Ray Cooney
Arsenic and Old Lace	Joseph Kesselring
Dial "M" for Murder	Frederick Knott

1994-1995

Jake's Women	Neil Simon
The Dining Room	A.R. Gurney
The Holly and the Ivy	
Ghosts	Henrik Ibsen
I Hate Hamlet	Paul Rudnick
Royal Gambit	Hermann Gressieker
A Month of Sundays	Bob Larbey
Send Me No Flowers	Norman Barasch & Carroll Moore
Charley's Aunt	Brandon Thomas
The Unexpected Guest	Agatha Christie

1995-1996

Lend Me a Tenor	Ken Ludwig
Lettice and Lovage	Peter Shaffer
Sorry, Wrong Chimney	Jack Sharkey & Leo Sears
Crown Matrimonial	Royce Ryton
The Curious Savage	John Patrick
The Sisters Rosensweig	Wendy Wasserstein
A Coat of Varnish	Ronald Millar
Out of Order	Ray Cooney
The Fourposter	Jan De Hartog
Witness for the Prosecution	Agatha Christie

1996-1997

Nunsense	Dan Goggin
Angel Street (Gaslight)	Patrick Hamilton
Auntie Mame	Jerome Lawrence & Robert E Lee
In Praise of Love	Terence Rattigan
Suddenly at Home	Francis Durbridge
King of Hearts	Jean Kerr & Eleanor Brooks
Pride and Prejudice (from the novel by Jane Austen)	Helen Jerome
Noises Off	Michael Frayn
Gentlemen Prefer Blondes	Anita Loos & Kristen Sergel
Towards Zero	Agatha Christie

1997-1998

A Funny Thing Happened on the Way to the Forum	Burt Shevelove, Larry Gelbart & Stephen Sondheim
Tea and Sympathy	Robert Anderson
My Three Angels	Sam & Bella Spewack
The Heiress	Ruth & Augustus Goetz
My Giddy Aunt	Ray Cooney & John Chapman
The Middle Ages	A.R. Gurney
The Trip to Bountiful	Horton Foote
Don't Dress for Dinner	Marc Camoletti

APPENDIX III

Editor's note: *Prologue* was written by Duncan Campbell Scott and spoken by Dorothy White at the opening of "The Little Theatre, Ottawa, Fourth of January 1928." This specially published momento was available at this auspicious event, which was also the opening night's performance of St. John Ervine's play, *Anthony and Anna*. A credit printed on the *Prologue* read:

THE MODERN PRESS, 126 QUEEN STREET
has produced this Prologue free of cost
and all the proceeds will be devoted to
the Ottawa Drama League. This generous
action is gratefully acknowledged…

Prologue

THE Prologue, in the days of long ago,
  Was set before the scene, designed to show
The drama's purpose or to explain away
The paltry ending of a tedious play.
It served to clear the stage of lingering beaux,
To warn the stalls that had begun to doze,
To drive the orange girls out of the pit,
To whet the mind with some display of wit.
Their foibles all are gone as fashions fade,
Like rose leaves of which potpourri is made;
Another age will find our ways outmoded,
Our manners droll, our tinsel all corroded;
But it may find some beauty in our fashions,
Some odour in our wreath of withered passions,
As all the glow and colour of Goldsmith's day
Is like a perfumed garland laid away.
Instead of powdered heads we have bobbed tresses,
Instead of ample skirts we have short dresses:
Thrilled by a knee now, by an ankle then,
The charm is constant—men are ever men.
Instead of link boys bold and candle-trimmers,
We have our switches, thousand watts and dimmers.
That brings me to my purpose—it is—in fine
To thank you all, to change old Omar's line,

II.

"Who *gave* the cash and let the credit go,"
Who changed these walls and made this pleasant show
Of comfort, who gave the audience room and ease,
Gave the stage manager a chance to seize
Modern effects, and brandish in his hand
The fitful lightning, bid it glow and stand
In pools of colour, gave the actor space
To don the costume and to paint the face,
Gave us in fact for all their varied uses
A temple for the loveliest of the Muses;
Our grateful thanks, and then again our thanks
To the loyal folk who filled the actors' ranks,
Who gave their time and talent without stint,
Fine ore and precious for the producer's mint;
Our thanks to him who made the perfect thing,
Beating the metal to a rounded ring;
To those who dressed the actors and the stage,
The doorkeeper, the prompter and the page,
Fair maids who left the dance, and lads the rink,
Forgetting social joys, to be the link
Between the patrons and the play. What we now see
Came from a seed planted courageously.
For treasured talent is a squandered thing;
What is despised is found a golden ring

III.

With a fine jewel set. For well I wis
When London was a town little as this,
What was thought lightly of, the casual play,
The swift amusement of a crowded day,
Has triumphed o'er the whirlwind and the strife
And come to mean the nobleness of life;
The crowning light and glory of that age
Centres on Marlowe's and on Shakespeare's stage.
What began here in humbleness and dearth
May make a noise around this careless earth,
Some national playwright may his plot unfold
Here—and some actor with a tongue of gold
Begin to speak upon this northern air,
If you, our generous patrons, will be fair,
And not refuse to reason or reflect,
Nor to find all our chosen plays suspect
That are not laughter full. Life on this earth
Is a rough turmoil tempered with small mirth,
Laughter comes dancing in, a gypsy elf,
Seeming all joy, sufficient to herself;
But as a rainbow gets her beauty from rain
And the purple rain-cloud; laughter's debt to pain
Is a dark background wet with tears.—And then,
Thank heaven, we have no "tired business men"

IV.

To be amused—but only persons of rude health
With latent vigour and sufficient wealth,
No Civil Servants of a delicate brood
Afflicted with a chronic lassitude,
They do not need subsistence of that kind,
The "funny plays" devoid of seeds and rind
Arid as fabled fruit of the Dead Sea,
But food for heroes—Let us now agree
To give you plays as various as life
Is various, plays of wonderment and strife,
Actions of poignancy and truth, revealing
The ever-tremulous deeps of human feeling;
Plays wherein tears and tenderness are furled
Like an autumn rose whose petals are seared and curled
With early frost, but whose heart is full of scent;
Dramas where the overtones of life are blent,
Where echoes fall and mystic colours shine,
Transmuted from an atmosphere divine,
Far-off and lonely. Then, not to be too strange,
Plays of the common life, the normal range
Of homely passions—where the tragedy
Is but a tempest in a pot of tea;
You could stand Shakespeare, perhaps in modern dress,
If not—then with a sort of modified stress
Upon tradiion—a modern ancientness;

V.

And then some farce, we promise that in sooth,
Whereon old Care may lose his wisdom-tooth.
And won't you let us choose some far-off day
Something bold, mischievous, risqué,
Thoroughly mondaine, bright, naughty and free
That no nice girl should take mamma to see,
Threats from the pulpit, letters in the press,
Puritan tea tables wiring S.O.S.
"And did she make that speech, I can't believe—!
That is the part was played by Molly Steeve.
Everyone says, my dear, its [sic] an awful show,
If that's the truth we'll simply have to go."
Of course I only say this just to tease,
Now let us be in earnest if you please:
As you all know 'tis our comfirmed intent
To foster native plays and actors, to invent
Beauty of scene and movement, and to enhance
The Joy of Life by the Drama and the Dance.
So criticise us always in good part,
For criticism is the tonic of art.
Be dumb, doubtful, indifferent, we are dead;
Gossip your full, talk us to life instead.
I may have bored you, but I've had my say,
Now let us laugh at St. John Ervine's play.

Afterword

Though the most be players, some must be spectators.
Ben Jonson
in *Timber, or Discoveries*
Made Upon Men and Matter

He that publishes a book runs a very great hazard,
since nothing can be more impossible
than to compose one that may secure
the approbation of every reader.
Miguel de Cervantes in *Don Quixote*